MW01152726

www.apsthebook.com
info@apsthebook.com

Ivan Fantin

Applied

Problem Solving

Book	Italian first edition © 2013
	English first edition © 2014
E-Book	Italian first edition © 2013
	English first edition © 2014

Designed by Ivan Fantin

For information, and to contact the author:
info@apsthebook.com

ISBN-13: 978-1499122282
ISBN-10: 1499122282

Index

PREFACE

Problem-solving is an every-day job: it is done by mothers when they have to cope with the sudden fever of their children combined with the need to go to work and manage the home.
It is done by managers who must respond promptly to everything that is not possible to schedule in advance.
It is also carried out by college students when they have to organise overlapping exams.
Furthermore it is performed by doctors when a diagnosis is ineffective and they must explore all possible causes of their patients' symptoms.
In short, since Adam ate the forbidden fruit, we have all had to deal with problem-solving.

Many methods have been developed to help people deal with problems in a structured way. Most of them have seen their development and application in business environments, where system complexity requires the most structured and scientific approach possible.
However, these methods often went out of control. The illusion of being able to achieve a perfect and comprehensive model has become a problem in itself, because they were too complicated to implement and manage.
"Problem Solving" has become a discipline that can be initiated and officiated only by so-called "gurus".

This book aims to pierce this veil of complexity that has enveloped "Problem Solving", by making the methodologies, tools and techniques needed to successfully deal with the ever-changing environment of the twenty-first century accessible to all. The current turbulent genetic situation of markets, economy and contemporary social systems have driven the author to seek and clarify approaches that will allow managers and, why not, all

individuals to better govern the process of creativity linked to the solution of problems.
The proposed concepts are not new and the model is not complicated. On the contrary, it's intentionally simple.
And that is where its strength lies: the attention to the applicability of the model rather than its elegance makes it a true innovative tool.

The author devotes a major part of the book to a variety of practical examples so that the reader can fully concentrate on how to apply the model rather than limit himself to the pure theory.
"Applied Problem Solving" collects years of experience of those who have had to use and adapt methods of problem solving in order to achieve operational excellence and management successes.
This whole experience has been transformed into a "toolbox" full of insights, ideas and innovative models useful to apply the art of Problem Solving.

The characteristic feature of capitalism is change and the constant search for new and more efficient solutions. It is therefore clear how structuring the problem, defining it, identifying its causes and knowing where to look, as well as being able to isolate the root causes, finding the solutions, measuring impact and sustainability, do not constitute a fleeting process, but a mandatory way to make our own lives and businesses sustainable in a complex and largely unknown environment.
The application of Problem Solving needs innovative approaches and methods that this volume aims to present in a clear, concise and effective way, also with the aid of several case studies of the modern company's strategic trajectory to win the competitive challenge.

Turin (Italy), July 2013

Francesco Rattalino
ESCP Europe Business School, Turin, Italy

PREFACE TO THE ENGLISH EDITION

Applied Problem Solving is a step by step guide for the reader to help them overcome daily problems they face within their home life or the workplace. Throughout this book the reader will be able to follow a structured approach which will help them recognise, analyse and remove the error between what is currently happening and the desired standard and ultimately stopping repetition.

The insight into these findings is all based on first hand experiences and proven tools and techniques. Therefore you the reader will be able to gain and benefit from these relevant experiences.

One of the reasons why I was inspired to be part of this APS book was my familiarity with the problem solving methodology; my current role is dedicated to continuous improvement, where I am intrigued and fascinated by what I have been part of.

I hope you all feel this passion as you take the migration towards becoming an accomplished problem solver.

Furthermore I express my true thanks to Ivan Fantin who helped and encouraged me to be part of this well presented and useful book of practices.

Cambridge (UK), April 2014

Julian Maya

Page intentionally left blank

0. INTRODUCTION

Goal	This chapter retraces the steps that have made the birth of the APS book possible.
Content	• The Problem Solving Skills in the Curriculum Vitae • The Practical Approach of the APS Methodology • The Structure of the Book

The Problem Solving Skills in the Curriculum Vitae

The Problem Solving skills, so frequently written in the professional profiles of a lot of people, are as much becoming one of the most skills that may be found in the Curriculum Vitae[1].
We are already good at solving problems, so why bother with this book?

All around us are people who have strong skills in problem solving, just wait a few moments and every problem will be solved easily by our friends, colleagues or family.
Is this true or is the reality different?

We may be unlucky, but who does have the feeling to be surrounded by capable problem solvers, please raise their hand. It may be possible that somebody is overestimating their own capabilities?

A survey by Forbes[2] confirmed my impression, indicating that, among the 10 qualities most sought by companies, the "complex problem solving", the "critical thinking" and the "judgment and decision making" selection criteria are present 90% of the times. Perhaps is this a confirmation that finding candidates capable of solving problems is not that easy?

To solve problems is quite different from firefighting here and there. To solve the problems we need a structured approach that addresses the problematic situations and traits so that the problem does not exist anymore.

---

1 Analysis reported in a study published on the blog of the recruiting firms Michael Page and Page Personnel, published on 1 February 2012 on the website www.espertilavoroecarriera.it

2 Forbes, the 10 skills That will get you hired in 2013, December, 2012, www.forbes.com/sites/meghancasserly/2012/12/10/the-10-skills-that-will-get-you-a-job-in-2013/ (visited in January 2013)

Problem Solving is not a common tool, or something you go and buy at the tool reseller. It is a structured mental model which allows you to deal systematically and effectively with problems.

Thanks to the method we will be able to identify problems, prioritise them, measure them, to find the causes and implement effective and lasting solutions to avoid the same problems from recurring in the future.

Quite often, those who consider themselves “problem solvers” only know a part of the process to be followed, they do not have a solid mental model, most of the times they get lost during the analysis and look for the guilty one, someone to blame. For these reasons they are not good in fixing the problem definitively and, as a consequence, they waste time arguing.

In addition to this, the severe shortage of not knowing how to identify the most effective solutions self-explains the reality in which we all live.

The problem solving methodologies have been around for several decades and they all have their strengths and weaknesses, along with being sufficiently reliable and effective.

The methodologies are .... not those who apply them.

Allow me this pun: if the application of problem solving methodologies does not guarantee the problem being solved, we have a problem to solve.

Starting from this last consideration, the Applied Problem Solving –APS– Methodology has been created. This is a practical methodology that can be easily applied to real issues, in which its simplicity and effectiveness, enforced by the focus on the execution of the solutions found is value added towards similar approaches.

The Practical Approach of the APS Methodology

If the application of problem solving methodologies does not guarantee the problem being solved, we have a problem to solve.

The challenge of making an extremely applicable theoretical model which can be applied in several different fields begun to passionate me. I found myself studying and deeply analyzing the most used methodologies[3] which I took part in a course as a student.

The more I was extending my knowledge, the more I understood that the theory illustrated by the methods and the way they are taught is not able to cancel the distance between the method and the person, between the theory and the practical application of it.

Whoever is in front of a problem at the end of the training, is very often still in trouble. It therefore happens that he cannot put in practice the teaching received, he swaps to a smaller-than-needed application phase and the results is not met.

The ability to demonstrate how the method works by using real cases brought by those who must learn, and the care of the effectiveness of solutions, it is even absent in most of the approaches.

This appeared to me to be more and more obvious until I said, "If the methods are all similar and have a lot of potential but cannot

[3] The most popular methods have been identified through the research of official publications, verifying the study schedules of business schools that prepare the Managers for the MBA, and have also been influenced by the work environments I have attended, in addition to including references historically adopted by almost all the publications, such as the Deming PDCA cycle: Plan, Do, Check, Act (Adjust).

find a practical application it is then normal that they are rarely used.

If the same methods show how to arrive at a solution but do not fully explain the "how to" implement the countermeasures, it is normal then that the solutions do not always work.
Let's solve the problem!"

Focusing on the applicability of the methodology provides an additional benefit that an overly theoretical model cannot manage. To fix problems is not a meeting room activity, a university hall approach, it's not just the theory we may study on the books. At least, it's not only that; the study is indeed necessary, but it is never the last phase, it rather constitutes a solid base.

The resolution of problems requires the ability to understand the context and the environment and then requires that people go to collect the evidences firsthand. Solving problems is a strenuous activity as it is to play with the practice, not just the theory.

However difficult it is a very effective and powerful activity, it is a plus compared to those who do not know how to apply the principle and method. It is an activity that will give you a lot of satisfaction.

Correctly applying problem solving will transform yourself into the *person who makes things happen.*

APS aims to fill this gap through a methodology that will necessarily be easy and logical to follow, while remaining very effective. In addition to this, APS will maintain a practical profile so that it becomes possible to apply the method in real scenarios.

In this way we will benefit from a model that follows an intuitive path and will also show its own effectiveness.

Correctly applying problem solving will transform yourself into the *person who makes things happen*

This added value is very important and is the differentiator that APS wants to offer. Did you know that a problem can also be solved by doing nothing? Do you know how to prioritise all the points that you have to fix? Do you know how to grasp and take advantage of the skills and potential of the people with whom you interface?

All these questions, once clarified will allow you to be individuals who, armed with a very solid mental model, will demonstrate abilities that are rare-to-find in other people.

The cover image of this book is a metaphor of a problem. If it has the correct size and is well identified, it will then be properly isolated from the rest, and easily eliminated.

The Structure of the Book

The book illustrates the APS model, enriched by real cases which have occurred and interesting ideas of other works, which are extraordinarily connected to problem solving despite not mainly dealing with the problem solving world.

In addition to this, it offers the opportunity to practice on real problems; it helps to gather ideas through examples of effective solutions and finally explains how to document the work done to maximise the consensus around the identified solutions, being very useful if problem solving is carried out in the professional field.

The ultimate goal is to convey a working method, effective and compatible with the methods that may be used by other people who are able to apply problem solving.

Thanks to this we can improve as individuals and as

professionals, as well as contribute positively to the groups we work with, to the pursuit of operational excellence.

At the end of the book you get an abstract graphic and a check list of two pages, which you can photocopy and use in your future problem solving sessions.

A heartfelt thanks to those who helped me to transform the first draft of this idea into the first edition of the Italian book: Tiziana Volpe, Francesco Rattalino, Giorgio Treichler and Stefano Ruffini, who already knew the APS methodology and who helped point out some perfect passages. Thanks also to Alda Marabini, Bruno Picoltrini, Stefano Brambilla, Santi Sottile and Davide Mosca who not knowing the APS method, enlightened me on the points to be improved because they were not clear enough.

A special mention is deserved by Julian Maya who helped me out in the heavy task of reviewing the English version, making it clearer and smoother to the readers.

Now let's dive into the APS method.

Happy reading and re-reading

Rho, Milan (Italy), April 2014

Ivan Fantin

Page intentionally left blank

1. A NEW CHALLENGE

Goal

Describe the situations in which APS can make a difference, including the identification of the common mistakes and describing the steps to better understand the situation. Some parallels with other works allow you to put problem solving at the center of many situations.

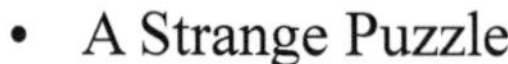

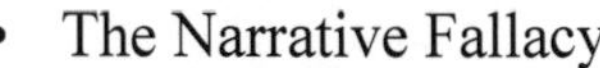

Content

- A Strange Puzzle
- Reorder Evidences
- The Narrative Fallacy
- The Identification Of The Real Problem
- Wrong Problem Definition
- Wrong Languages
- Stop The Complaints
- Changing Behaviour
- Decompose The Problem

A Strange Puzzle

Imagine this scenario: you've arrived at home and, after hurrying up your domestic chores, you can dedicate time to the new gift that you have made yourself: a nice puzzle to solve, releasing tension and relaxing, one of your favorite hobbies.

You open the box and realise that it is a puzzle a bit special: the tiles do not have any contoured sides, they have straight sides and are shaped perfectly square; moreover, on the box cover the final image that the puzzle will show once completed is missing.

How can you solve this puzzle?

You are dealing with a problem that requires the "Applied Problem Solving" approach, a puzzle that requires higher resolution capabilities, a puzzle that will give you a new level of satisfaction once completed.

Fig: 1.1: A strange puzzle

The box of the puzzle normally contains all the tiles mixed together.

To place the pieces correctly together is critical to begin to distinguish the first small portions of the image.

The box of the traditional puzzle shows the final image on the cover; without it would be very difficult to identify the first group of tiles, then it would be equally difficult to control the situation and see if we are proceeding correctly. Without the photo on the cover, the strategy would become a very un-satisfying guesswork. Consequently, this would reduce greatly the chances of being able to complete the puzzle and get the final image.

What happens when you have to solve a problem is very similar to working on this type of puzzle, without the final image on the cover of the box. By having only tiles that are hard to pair and unshaped, the joint between them must be verified by logic rather than by attempts. We need a method.
And, in real problems, is not said that the tiles are all there.

Reorder Evidences

Without a solid strategy we will go on randomly, resulting in an image that may not the correct one but it is simply the image easiest to compose. If the puzzle is the scenario of a problem to solve, the problem will not be solved. In other words, understanding how to organise the evidences of the problem is of paramount importance to clarify the problematic situations.

Understanding how to organise the evidences of the problem is of paramount importance to clarify the problematic situations

We are saying that the problem can be addressed by rearranging the scenery as if it were a puzzle of unconnected, incomplete and missing information, from which we must derive the story.

Only by working on this we will understand what happened when the problem occurred. To collect the majority of tiles possible it is necessary to tell, or be told, what is happening and what has happened, in great detail leaving no stone unturned, but especially without interpreting the occurrence. It is important not to proceed with quick (mis)interpretations.

Thanks to the emotional distance that must be maintained, it will be much easier to avoid prejudices and gather as much evidences which can be collected, just one for each tile. However, not having the picture on the box cover, and not being able to take advantage of the geometric joints on each tiles side, the only way to compose the final image is to place each tile of evidence according to the only logical that we have available: the time.
For convenience we can use colored sticky notes in place of the tiles, to easily move them if necessary.

We need to assess when the evidence, represented by each sticky note, happens in comparison to the other tiles. This should not be done in absolute terms, indicating the day and time, but in relative terms, indicating whether the evidences of the tile that you have in your hands happened before, after or during what is written on the other tiles that have already been placed on the table of the puzzle.

Think about your problem, tell yourself about the story that you wish to describe and then prepare one sticky note for each piece of evidence you have, without asking at this stage whether it is important or not for the purposes of the having the problem solved.

The Narrative Fallacy

History, the one we study at school, is based on the events and the time when they have mutually occurred, not only on the absolute moment in which they occurred, right?
Well, if the time line guides the events of a story, for us this confirms that the joints of each tile of the problem are not based on the shape but depends on the historical moment in which the

event shown on each tile has occurred.

Unfortunately, history may be boring and hard to remember. For this reason screenplay, novels or simply stories contain a certain amount of time reordering omissions and/or changes to some of the details.

This is not a case, it is a strategy: it is meant to make the story interesting and compelling, even if thought-of-fact creates a distortion of reality.

The consequence is that the same event can be narrated in different ways that bias its meaning. Causes and effects are rearranged, influencing the way of thinking of the recipient of the story. The result is having a compelling story to tell that goes away significantly from the actual facts.

Information, especially when collected in retrospect, appear disconnected from each other, are difficult to obtain, store and rearrange. This theory has been very well illustrated by Nassim Nicholas Taleb in his book "The Black Swan" where it is defined as "narrative fallacy"[4]. This is illustrated by the following explanation: the memory of the people and the arrow of time are sometimes confused. The narrative plays a dangerous role as it can change the events that have occurred by packing them in a form easy to remember. In these cases dominates the later reconstruction of the logical thread that links the events.

The danger is that the story is affected by the changes, the additions and the reconstructions, that serve only to make the narration sleek, neglecting the truth of the content and giving the meaning that best fits with the little information that you have, and suddenly not all.
This drives mistakes in anyone who is looking to discover

[4] Nassim N. Taleb, *The Black Swan. The Impact of the Highly Improbable,* Random House, 2007

the real truth behind the story, regardless if it is collected through a report, a newspaper article or any summary of the facts carried out in retrospect, when it is easier to know the effects and not the causes.

Taleb summarises by saying that the people continue to *"retell past events in the light of what seems to give them a logical sense after they have occurred."*

The Problem Solver, who wants to solve problems, cannot afford to fall into this trap!

The Identification of the Real Problem

In the next few pages of this book you will learn a great way of breaking down the story we have been talking about into a number of tiles. We will go on reassembling the tiles according to a timeline that will allow focusing on the key points of the problem to be solved, a crucial step in order to proceed with the additional analysis.

If the real problem is not properly identified the risk is very high: in all likelihood you will work to solve a false problem and perhaps a false annoyance; that will create the frustration of not being able to fix the situation.

To tell at a glance if we are in a risky situation requires that kind of sensitivity illustrated in the following paragraphs:

- Identify any definition mistake
- Detect errors of language
- Stop the complaints
- Changing behaviour
- Decompose the problem

Wrong Problem Definition

It happens quite often to observe people jumping to conclusions or believing that they have understood the problem but in

reality the situation is not clear at all.
Who makes that mistake ends up in investing time and money in doing activities that are unnecessary or irrelevant with the problem that he was trying to solve.

And the problem remains.

The problem solver must develop a sixth sense to detect all scenarios in which may exist the danger of having the problem poorly defined, falling then into the biggest mistake possible when attempting to solve a problem. Albert Einstein said that if he ideally should have given one hour to save the world he would have spent 55 minutes defining the problem, and 5 minutes to solve it.

> Jumping to conclusions means investing time and money in useless activities

As Problem Solvers we need to learn to doubt those who, in describing the situations, are always talking about problems here and there, indicating that the problem is "something" that they do not actually know in the extension and in the context.

These people often transform the problem solving analysis into sports-bar debates, in typical post-game verbal conflicts, in which all are coaches and everyone has their winning solution, the perfect strategy for the substitutions, and the solution to a problem they do not know in deep.

Whoever would trust and link the results of the national sport team to play the scheme proposed from time to time in every bar on the street, that at the end of each game provide expert tips on how to win all the games (especially those already played and lost already)?

Julio Velasco[5] is very good at describing these mixed

5 Julio Velasco (born February 9, 1952 in La Plata, Argentina) is a

> phenomenon that lie between the Leadership and the world of sports competitions. He says, rightly, that the explanations are an activity that only losers have to do.
> Who wins the game has won; full stop! The loser must spend time himself in explanations.
> Making a careful identification of the problem is critical to get back to winning, otherwise you stumble into new defeats and you will tend to shift the blame on someone, without resolving the problems that led to losing the game itself.

Wrong Language

Jumping to conclusions is dangerous. Your ability to identify potentially dangerous situations will improve greatly if you become very sensitive and receptive to all scenarios in which there is an abuse of misspelled words or an abuse of terms that denote a wrong assessment of the current situation.

The terms shown in the following table, including their variations and/or synonyms, may be used to identify situation that are potentially at risk due to lack of knowledge of the problem to be solved:

Accusations:	- They... - You Guys... - You... - He/She...

professional volleyball coach from Argentina, who guided the Italian national men's team to several successes in the 1990s. After the 1996 Summer Olympics, where the Italians won silver, he switched to the Italian women's team (1996–1997). In 2011, Velasco was signed as the head coach of the Iran men's national team. He is also well known as a motivational public speaker for business organisations

Lack of Evidences:	- Sometimes... - Maybe.... - I've heard.... - In my experience... - Good... - Bad... - Rubbish...
Jump to Conclusions:	- We miss... - The problem is... - We need.... - The point is....
Lack of Leadership:	- Let's hope that....

Fig: 1.2: Words which may show that a problem solving approach is needed

These groups of statements constitute a signal, the signal that tells us we are in a situation in which:

- we are looking for a guilty party rather than looking for a solution (Accusations)
- the situation is unclear (Lack of Evidences, Lack of Leadership)
- we are trying to act randomly; it seems that the important thing is to do something, no matter what (Jump to Solutions and Lack of Leadership).

So the problem, again, remains unsolved.

Stop the Complaints

A further signal consists of the criticisms and complaints about what happened in the past, often ignoring the reasons. The use of our time to bring up past events to criticise decisions and behaviour is not a good investment.

The people find immediate relief in criticising what has happened, but in the long run, this has a negative effect: it helps to increase the sense of frustration and helplessness against problems that should be solved by "those responsible"[6] without understanding that, very often, "those responsible" are us.

On this point, Julio Velasco teaches that the best progress with his teams came when he banned every team member to talk about the past, indicating that the only way to invest all the resources that you have, is to search for a way to do things in a better way in the future. With this compromise he has (perhaps) reduced the speed to identify solutions, but at the same time the risk that the members of his team may fall into controversy on the mistakes already made in the past, without contributing to their resolution, has been completely eliminated.

If you do what you've always done you'll get what you've always gotten

The book Toyota Kata[7] vividly illustrates this situation: if you do not have the time to convince people of the goodness of a new method, you have to start working to change their behaviour, so they can understand why the changes are necessary.
In some cases, the theory is not the best way to begin; you should start with some activity, and then explain why they were carried out in that way; after the change is made and the results are visible and real, the doubts of those skeptic are easily removed.

6 "Those Responsible" is often referred to as the one who has the authority, the means and resources to make decisions about unclear issues. Often, very often, this person does not exist or is not well identified because the task could be responsibility of more than one individual and so no one does anything. In all these cases, "those responsible" is us, we just need to start doing rather than criticising.

7 Mike Rother, *Toyota Kata: Managing People for Improvement, Adaptiveness, and Superior Results,* McGraw-Hill, 2009

Changing Behaviour

"If you do what you've always done
you'll get what you've always gotten"

This quote is sometimes attributed to Henry Ford, founder of Ford Motor Company, or to Anthony Robbins, a motivational PNL speaker, as well as to the physician Albert Einstein.

Regardless of those who first formulated, this quote contains a very enlightening meaning about the repeatability of the results related to the same actions. The people who are able to exercise their leadership skills have understood this concept very well, and have realised that measuring the results of their actions is instrumental to gaining the best results.
Real leaders have identified what is the behaviour that allows them to exercise their magnetism over others. Around these habits they usually search for perfection slightly changing and adapting their behaviour.

Problem solving skills helps to show what you are capable of; just working with the focus to perform well, and paying attention to follow the methodology, the results will come.
Communicating and communicating is not enough to make us achieve this goal. We need to work on changing the behaviour, which we will go into more depth in the section of the book relating to solutions to problems, in which we will also see how you can get results in changing the behaviour of others.

"When to communicate is
the only solution to your problem,
be prepared to communicate the failure"

Changing the behaviour of others, even though it first requires the change of how we behave, has always been the most effective conduct in nature, the one instinct against whom it is difficult to oppose.
An animal or a plant, when very flashy and bright in colors, will

be hardly pleasant to eat, and the predators know this very well. For the prey, to adopt a behaviour of visibility, drives the behaviour of predators in a much more effective way than a hypothetical sign with written "do not eat me, I'm not good."
The leaders knows this very well and frequently take advantage of this powerful trick.

John Shook, author of "A3 Managing to Learn", in his newsletter described the phenomenon and proposed how to deal with it, thanks to a highly effective phrase:

"When you see good leadership,
follow it, if you wish.
If you do not see it, take it if you wish.
If not, do not complain"[8]

Decompose the Problem

Many of the problem solving methods suggest breaking the big problem into smaller problems to make it more manageable. Although this type of approach is very valuable, it is not sufficient to solve negative scenarios permanently. The real advantage of breaking down the big problems into smaller problems, for those who have a robust and reliable method, is based on the reduction of the problem size to ensure that the size of each piece is comparable to the dimension of the experiences that each of us possesses.

This is the same logic behind the creation of the WBS in projects (Work Breakdown Structure) in which the project is divided into many work-packages.
The ultimate benefit is to manage phases of the project through activities (Tasks) that have a dimension and a complexity that is compatible with the capabilities of the team members or groups.

[8] From John Shook's Newsletter of April, the 21st, 2013 "*Lead from the Front, Lead from Behind*" in which the lacks of the leadership are covered.

Let's see what it means to "break down the problem" in the APS method. The problem must be seen as a story that you can tell, a story that can be made up of different pieces of a puzzle, where each tile contains one and only one brick of the story, one evidence only.
The decomposition of the problem is of fundamental importance, and to master this technique is a key quality to becoming excellent problem solvers.

The mechanism is simple and powerful: the problem must be told by those who know enough elements (including ourselves if it is the case). During the storytelling, the problem solver (the one who wants to solve the problem) must quickly take note of each piece of evidence by using sticky notes, one per each element, without worrying about dependencies on other elements at this stage, and possibly without influencing the narrator.

Let's take an example: the problem we want to describe is the scenario in which you frequently drain the car battery; this suddenly happens during parking time, when we forget to turn the headlights off, and because of this, we often arrive late to appointments and we have to make excuses, we have to postpone meetings, to refrain from interesting events and to justify our poor punctuality, receiving reprimands.

The frustration raises and we lose opportunities, therefore this constitutes a problem to solve. The decomposition of the evidences leads to the following list of puzzle tiles, which for convenience we can physically wrote down on sticky notes as already pointed out:
- Low battery
- Headlights left on
- Loss of opportunities
- Delays
- Frustration
- Reproaches
- Justifications

- Time-shortages

After the first few times you will learn not to neglect any of the elements of the story, elements that in this first phase should not be evaluated or judged. It does not matter if they are disconnected or are irrelevant, it will be in later stages of the application of our method in which to detect if there are unnecessary elements.

2. THE ARROW OF TIME *(when)*

Goal

Guide the reader through the stages of reconstructing the history in order to correctly identify and effectively address the problem to be solved

Content

- The Arrow of Time
- The Cause-Effect Relationship
- The Problem Tree
- The Measurement of the Problem
- The Tree of Hypotheses

Fig: 2.1: The Doughnut of APS: When

Figure 2.1 shows the first phase of the APS methodology doughnut, the graphical representation of all the required steps to perform. As you proceed with the steps of the method we will see that the Doughnut will be enriched with simple details.

The purpose of the Doughnut is to split the method into seven easy steps plus one, and in each stage symbolically represent the activities to be carried out.
In this way we will always have at hand a clear map of what activities are needed and at which point in the process we are.
Let's figure out what it means to have a tree in the first phase of our work method.

The Arrow of Time

The tiles of the puzzle already used as examples in the first chapter are of fundamental importance because they allow us to reconstruct the history by maintaining a certain emotional distance from the events, even by those who are directly involved.
We start by placing the evidences on a timeline, a vertical line from bottom -the past-, to top -the present-. All evidences must

be positioned on the arrow on the basis of when they happened. It is not necessary to indicate the date and time for each one, nor it is important the absolute position they take on the tree model.

It is the relationship between evidences, which represent the relative moment by which every evidence happened, that tells the story.

Placing the sticky notes according to the time scale, from the bottom upwards, as they get closer to the present, two things generally happen:

1) whoever tells the story of the problem starts evaluating the events more objectively
2) whoever hears the story of the problem collects precious elements that allow him to apply the method in a surprisingly more effective way, even if he has collected previous experiences on the topic.

It is like getting lost in the middle of a maze: if we cannot climb on something to raise our point of view, we will never have the perception of how huge the maze is and what kind of strategy can be adopted to reach the exit.

Fig: 2.2: The Arrow of the Time

We proceed as follows: you draw an arrow upwards on a sheet

of paper; this arrow is the time line with the present in the upper part and the past at the bottom. The future has no place on this model because we're not working on assumptions but on real evidences, events that have already happened or are happening right now.

Then we place the sticky notes starting at the top of the arrow by stitching the most recent evidence we have, organising vertically one below the other as they happened at different times in the story, and horizontally those events that happened at the same time and are parallel to each other.

Here are placed all the evidences that normally do not depend on exactly each other but they arise from the same underneath cause, they are triggered by the same event

Fig: 2.3: The Arrow of the Time populated of evidences

The Cause-Effect Relationship

With this exercise we are able to create a map in which each sticky note has the characteristic of both cause and effect; if they are in a vertical relationship that means they are consistent, while if they are side by side that means they are providing a major completeness.

By acting in this way we can also start to realise if the information we have are complete or not. Moreover, we can address in this case the wrong human approach of believing more in a good story rather than believing in a simple-but-true list of unconnected evidences. Knowing this mistake we can manage to avoid the human tendencies which believe more in a good than in a real story.

Now there is an extra factor to consider since we are breaking down the story into individual elements to exclude the cosmetic part of it and keep only what is real.

Let's figure out if there are any shortcomings which can be highlighted by changing our way of thinking, as demonstrated by Wason in 1960 with the test of the 2-4-6 triplet.
Wason proposed to a group of individuals to find the rule that lies behind the construction of the 2-4-6 triplet asking a group of people to propose other triplets. He then would have answered just "yes" or "no" if the proposal had complied with the rule created by him, the one with which he had built the 2-4-6 triplet.
Individuals participating in this test normally come to the conclusion that the rule is something like "even numbers 2 to 2", or "add 2 to the previous number", without identifying the true rule is very simple and trivial: "growing numbers".
The explanation of this phenomenon lies in the fact that people normally tend to confirm their hypotheses rather than to seek a way to discredit those to verify if the

assumptions keep on surviving. Even if the other proposals made sense, this shows how easy is for the humans to complicate simple things.

Let's change our approach!

Let us strive to look for evidences to show that our theories are wrong. This procedure will avoid making mistakes. The humanly physiological attitude is to look only for evidences to the facts that our theory is correct; this will make us lose sight of the truth.

The Problem Tree

Many theories, as far as outlandish, can be confirmed by at least one test in their favor. But there are few theories that are resistant to evidences against them, and those are theories that say the truth, at least until proven otherwise[9].

people tend to confirm their hypotheses rather than to seek a way to discredit those and verify if they resist

The overall positioning of the sticky notes typically assumes a tree shape, in which the crown, composed of branches and leaves, metaphorically represents the young portion of the tree. That's the part that contains all the evidences of the same problem, the most visible evidences, which is something that happens also with the foliage of real trees that can be seen even from a distance.

9 *in dubio, pro reo:* from Latin, until proven otherwise, the accused must be considered innocent. Similarly, a theory is true until proven otherwise. The humans, which like more the success than the failure, tend to find evidences for their theories rather than evidences that the hypothesis are incorrect. The problem solver instead, which bases his success on the reconstruction of the truth to solve problems, will be successful when, giving up the satisfaction with an easy confirmation of a wrong theory, will do the opposite pursuing the highest satisfaction of having the problem solved.

As in all the shapes in the form of a tree there is a typical shrinkage in the trunk area; this represents the link that the leaves have with the ground.

The trunk is a visible part of the tree that has the characteristic function of supporting and providing lifeblood to the leaves. It is the anatomical part of the tree that focuses upon itself and has the responsibility to support and feed the branches and foliage. The model of a “problem tree” shows the crown as all the available evidences that confirm there is a problem and we have to work on that.

Fig: 2.4: The Problem Tree

For this reason the trunk of the tree represents the problem in our model made up of the sticky notes. We are just saying that the problem is represented by what is written on one of the notes that are attached on the trunk.

This pattern is widely adopted by many problem solving methodologies and has close similarities with the fishbone diagrams of Ishikawa, especially in the area of the trunk and roots.

It's a very useful model that allows you to display the first phases of problem solving, otherwise called “problem setting”; this becomes a natural link to the “problem finding” activities. This is a great way to simplify the methodological approach to solving the problem. Whether the problem is complex or not, the method should remain as simple as possible, this is what guarantees its effectiveness.

Should you ask yourself: "Do I always have to draw the tree for every problem?", then the answer is: "it depends".
It depends on the complexity of the situation and what your ability is to carry out the reconstruction of the tree, even if it is only mentally.

Having a written record of the situation is of strategically importance if we are working with other people, it helps to share the "vision" of the problem before proceeding.

The Measurement of the Problem

Let's now see how to select the best sticky note among those that falls on the trunk of the tree in our model.

the problem is best represented by what is written in one of the sticky notes on the trunk of the tree

Before reaching this answer we have to think a moment on the similarity to the tree. The fact that we select a note in the trunk area is a huge advantage for those who must solve the problem.
The tree trunk is an area where the links between the underlying causes and the upwards effects are simplified, where all causes flow and from which all the effects start.
It’s like a bottleneck, like the roadblock

that the police put in place to stop a fugitive so they force all traffic in a single lane to observe the passengers of each vehicle. Overseeing this area is the best and most effective approach to monitor the situation.

A measurement made to the area of the trunk is enough to provide information on the problem; in other words this is the measurement that best represents the problem itself.
And it is also fully exhaustive.

At this point it becomes important to understand that the problem must be something measurable, highlighting one of the key concepts of problem solving: If a problem cannot be measured then it is not a problem!

Someone may argue that the problem can be present even in the absence of a measurement that represents it.

a problem, if it is not measurable, is not a problem

However, we must consider that most of the problems have multiple shades, they are not all black or white, they are different shades of gray, and between these gradients there are those which are acceptable and not acceptable; moreover, between past, present and future, the criterion of acceptance of shades can change.

As a consequence, to define the extent of the problem it is necessary to indicate which values are normal, acceptable, and which are not. Only then, after having stated with certainty which are the desired conditions we can move on with the problem solving next phases.

In the trunk of the tree flows the lifeblood to all the leaves. It is in the trunk of the tree that we must look for the metric[10],

[10] Metric stands for what is chosen as reference to check and monitor the performance of a system. The "performance metrics" are a way to measure the activities and the performances of an organisation.

possibly just only one, the one that represents the problem in the best way.
We can therefore say that we have a problem and that the problem can be represented by the metric we have identified.

The problem solver must always ask himself, without exception, the question: "how do I measure this problem?"

In the absence of a measurement a value of acceptance will never be possible to assess a problem as a "problem solved". In this field, the medicine has made enormous progresses to try to translate the discomfort of patients into something measurable so you can talk about normality, a finally solved problem, or about serious conditions, stable disease or healing.

A problem that cannot be measured cannot be solved
-by definition- it is, if anything, an opportunity or a challenge but it is not a problem that can be solved.
To set ourselves with a measurable target, after having spent time and money to rebuild the scenario, it is a critical step for the proper setting of the entire problem solving work package.

Let's say we have a problem to solve. According to our definition there is a situation that does not meet a standard of desirable consequences. It's a situation that needs to be changed, because we want to change the outcome of what is happening.

Identifying which is the result of the current non-acceptable effect and what is the desired result, the acceptable one, allows us to define a goal, to describe a moment in the future and a specific situation in which we can say that the problem will be considered solved. Should that be highly or poorly ambitious that does not matter at this stage.

The constraint to make the problem measurable allows us to seize an opportunity. Knowing that the best metrics are placed in the trunk, we can begin to take advantage of having spent

time and effort in building the tree of the problem.
We will have to select between the sticky notes which are closer to the middle of the trunk, to pick up the easiest to measure. It is important to choose a metric cleverly, one that is easy to measure because the future efforts should and must be addressed to solve the problem, not to measure it (!). For this reason it must be an easy to understand and easy to perform measurement.

"How much fever do you have?"

At this point we are able to *transform a compelling but confusing narrative in a puzzle of evidences, properly rearranged on the vertical scale of time, that assumes the shape of a tree, in which the trunk lays the evidence which will become the metric to define the problem and verify the resolution.*

The most purists might argue that a problem remains un-measurable if we deliberately choose an evidence "of convenience" to monitor the situation; although this observation appears correct in theory, at least, the logic and the method show that measuring any aspect on the trunk of the tree appears to be a representative measurement of the problem itself, we just have to pick up the easiest to perform.

We are saying, in other words, that our problem can be represented by the chosen measure.

It would be like discussing whether it is more appropriate to measure the speed in kilometers per hour, in meters per second, in miles per hour or minutes per kilometer or mach. What matters is to identify any method of measuring the speed that allows the measuring of the problem.

If I decide to arrive on time for an appointment my average speed on the highway must be not lower than a certain value, no matter how I measure my ability to move, it is important that I define the goal, which is the value of average speed to hold, and I have to measure (monitor) the speed several times during the trip to confirm if I'm keeping the ideal speed so I can restore it if necessary.

Let's take another example: assume that at this time a cold is spreading in our community and who becomes affected feels discomfort and loses concentration, which limits his productivity and even force him to not go to work.

Who gets contaminated, additionally, feels bone pain accompanied by fever, a situation that normally indicates the presence of a bacterial or viral infection.

The decomposition of the problem leads to the following list of evidences:
- Sickness
- Lack of concentration
- Bone pain
- Fever
- Low productivity
- Bacterial infection
- Viral infection
- Inability to go to work
- Cold (disease)

These evidences, when re-ordered according to the time scale give once again a tree shape such as the following:

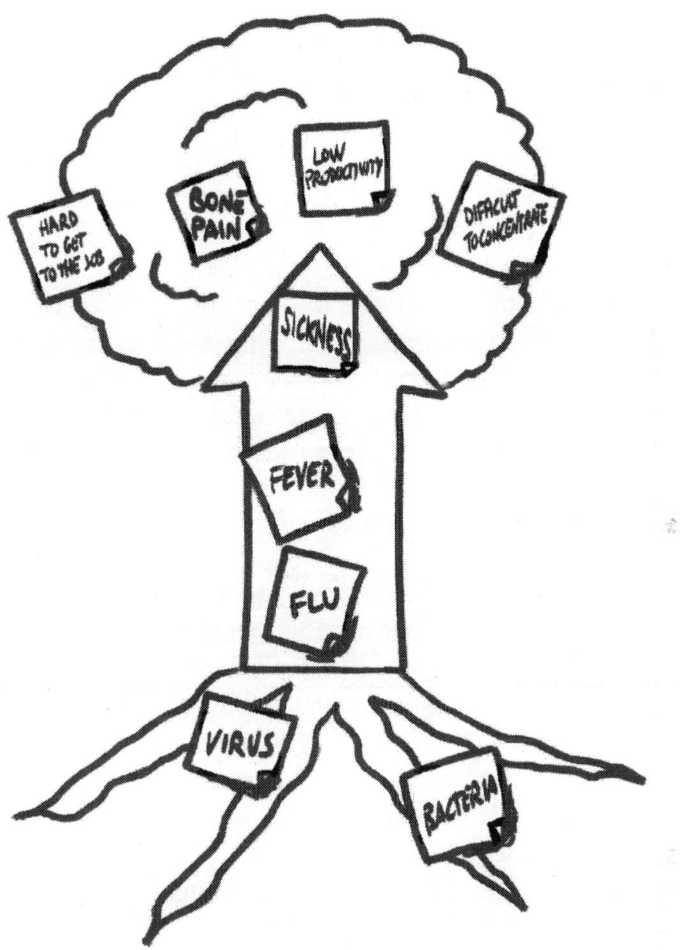

Fig: 2.5: The Flu Problem Tree

Is the tree model only useful to describe a known situation which has happened already, or can also be used to understand the ongoing problem even if the evidences are not sufficient?

The tree can be used for two different scenarios.
The first scenario is the reconstruction of the real story that is supported by real evidences.
The second scenario is the reconstruction of the most probable history, when unfortunately, we have no real evidences or those

that we do have are not completely reliable (it happens when you cannot get access to all the elements of the problem, or when you try to act in a preventative manner of probable problems that we would expect may happen).

In these two cases we refer, respectively, to the problem tree or to the hypotheses tree.

In the above example, the fact that we are looking for a measurable item in the trunk area allows us to focus in the area where we have flu and fever. In the upper area of evidences we might mistakenly identify as measurable the "productivity" sticky note, but this would lead to a mistake: it is not correct to say that the productivity (how fast and effective we are in doing our job) is the right measure of the discomfort caused by the flu.
The productivity can depend on many other factors and is definitely not a significant way to measure the body disease if it is lower than expected. We could then indicate that staying in bed may become the measurable evidence, but there may be other reasons that affect my inability to go to work that are not related to the body disease.

In this simple context, it is clear that the problem is "having the flu" and that without the influence we would not have had all the symptoms; it is also clear that the way I measure this problem could be, for convenience, the body temperature. This is a unique and practical approach to measure the situation by comparing the body temperature with the acceptable range.
Similarly, the definition of what are the limits of acceptability is fundamental for the problem, to identify a way to determine if the cold is gone without having to measure all the evidences one by one.
If I want to lower the body temperature what is my goal? Which temperature do I have to reach?

The problem tree allows us to understand what happened thanks to the collection of sufficient real evidences.

What if, however, we do not have enough real evidences to proceed with our investigations?
In such cases it is possible to work with the hypotheses tree.

The Hypotheses Tree

In all those cases where we do not have enough evidences and we don't know enough facts about the problem to be solved, it is not possible to complete the tree by using the fewer available items which compose the final puzzle.
In this case, we have only a few sticky notes and we cannot complete the final picture.

The risk of falling into the already described scenario, called "narrative fallacy" is very high. In these cases it is therefore necessary to interpret the situation in order to reconstruct the missing evidences, running a higher risk of making a mistake. In these cases, however it is convenient to start working with the few available sticky notes, proceeding by hypothesis with the reconstruction of the missing tiles to reconstruct the tree.
But this is not enough, each one of the hypothesis must be subjected to a destructive test, it must be subjected to a critical analysis by reasoning, to highlight those that do not stand up to criticism and therefore are not useful in the reconstruction of the final image. In such cases we have to eliminate them from the tree, as suggested by Wason in the trial of the 2-4-6 triplet.

Working with the tree of hypotheses is an equally effective method if done correctly, but more and more effort is needed by the individuals or the team that works there: it is much easier to look for evidences rather than arguing and browsing all known ways to destroy them.

The tiles that resist to critical reasoning or that are sufficiently robust have to be considered reasonable and relevant and need to be tested further in the MECE test (Mutually Exclusive,

Collectively Exhaustive) which requires what follows[11].
In the lower part of the tree, where the trunk is divided into more roots, the sticky notes, which are one beside the other, must be Mutually Exclusive, that means they must not be duplicates of each other but must be evidences that makes sense to consider in parallel.

This is not over, these sticky notes also need to be comprehensive in their entirety and must be Collectively Exhaustive, because they have to fully support the story without leaving holes here and there, by eliminating the doubt we may have not considered all the possible causes.
Research techniques of all the hypotheses are so that the final result is enough to complete and meet the MECE test. These techniques will be discussed later in the book as they will have the same approach that will be used when we have to collaborate in searching for solutions to the problem.

Some of these techniques are shared with the project risk management methodologies. Risks on projects are nothing more than hypotheses about the possible problems we may face in the future. The problem solving methodology contains tools for identification of the risks and proposals for managing or mitigating their effects.

Should we think of problem solving such a project to reduce the gap, we can easily take advantage of the same techniques to the final goal. Consider the possible causes of an unknown situation as all of the risks that may reside on roots of our hypotheses tree. Where we have no real evidences to work with on the Problem Tree, we have to move to the Hypotheses Tree scenario, in which we act like the Project Manager who is

---

11 MECE means, Mutually Exclusive, Collectively Exhaustive is proposed by McKinsey through the consultancy activities and is deepened in the following book: Rasiel, Ethan; Friga, Paul. *The McKinsey Mind: Understanding and Implementing the Problem-Solving Tools and Management Techniques of the World's Top Strategic Consulting Firm* (1 ed.). McGraw-Hill, 2001.

considering in advance the possible risks of his/her project.
There is only one difference: for us the problem was already built, and we can support with great certainty which are the risks that have come true. In other words, while working on the assumptions we are able to look for confirmation or immediate denial, thanks to the fact that the events may have already happened. To manage the risks of the project is more difficult as you try to predict negative situations, not knowing if and when they might happen.

Page intentionally left blank

3. WHAT HAPPENED *(what)*

Goal

To learn how to correctly define the problem to proceed to the next steps of investigation of the causes, avoiding as much as possible to work on the wrong problem

Content

- The Problem Definition
- The Run Charts
- Caused Problems and Created Problems
- Mixed Type Problems

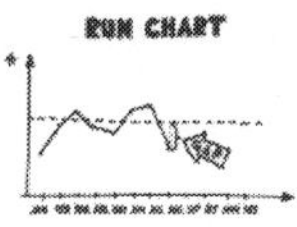

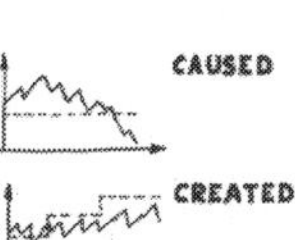

Fig: 3.1: The APS Doughnut: What

The Problem Definition

As we've already understood, the definition of the goal of the problem is the fundamental step to problem solving. This step must become mandatory in the definition of the problem.

The Goal is the value which the chosen metric has to show to indicate that the problem has been resolved, that the level of acceptability for the entire scenario has been reached. It's the value of the metric that indicates the elimination of the gap between where we were and where we wanted to be. It is the normal body temperature we want to reach when we are sick with a fever.

It's a big step forward, we started from a situation where it was not clear what was going on, we have reconstructed the logic and the scenery until we found out what is the best way to measure the problem using numbers.

The complexity has been reduced a lot.

Now we have to reach our target by measuring it just with the chosen metric to represent the problem.

The problem is the Gap between where we are and where we want to be

This is the way to reconsider the problem to a more manageable size.
The ability to express the problem numerically provides further opportunities to draw a chart that shows the evolution of the situation. The chart has the feature to quickly communicate the trends and the numerical differences. This chart is also called a "run chart".

The Run Charts

Expressing a complex problem on a chart (only one) is in itself a small but useful victory. A situation so complex that used to look like a tangled knot of facts and consequences now corresponds to a line on a sheet of paper from which we can guess not only the trend and the duration, we can also compare it with the expected result and the goal, which is normally represented as a dotted line.

The trend allows us to understand if the situation is deteriorating more and more, or if the line is farther and farther away from the objective as we take measurements, and also allows us to identify when the situation has become unacceptable.

This simplification is the key for being able to continue in our problem solving phases and this will not be the only simplification we'll see. To simplify the situation is an element of victory in solving problems.

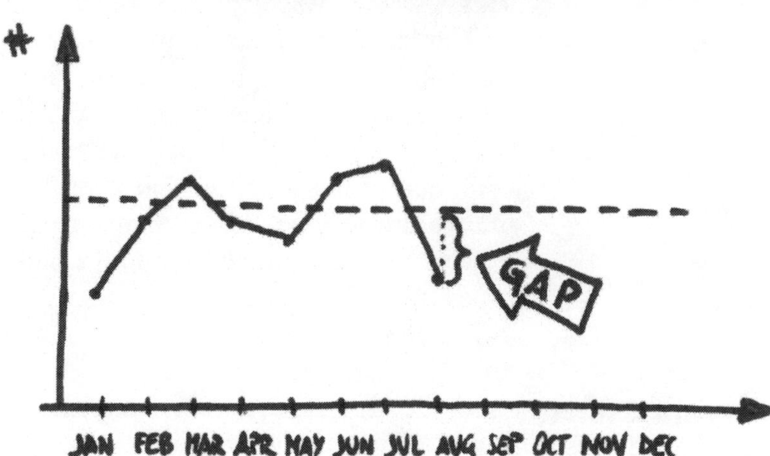

Fig: 3.2: Run Chart

The run charts are relatively easy to build, especially by following these few ground rules:

1. The "actual" line of the run chart is a continuous line representing the value that the indicator assumed so far in time and cannot extend in the future.

2. The "target" line is dashed and may not even be available for past periods, but must express clearly where we want to go in the future.

3. The target line can also express a gradual attainment of the final target, especially when you realise that the goal cannot be met immediately but you should gradually move towards the final result.
   Often the reason is tied to a certain response delay of the metric as a result of the actions that we are going to take (increased sales, reduced waste, increased punctuality, accumulation of savings, etc.) In other words, it can be a straight (diagonal or horizontal) line or a stepped line.

4. The width of the chart must be sufficient to contain meaningful information about the data of the actual line from the previous periods, plus a sufficient number of future periods in which the goal line is stabilised and meaningful (so it must contain many future periods in cases which the achievement of the final goal is gradual)

5. A chart must always respond to the need to be quickly interpretable, in other words it must have the units of measure on both axes, horizontal and vertical, it must use the available space to highlight the significant variations without falling off the scale, and must also highlight the four values by which the problem is described: actual, goal (or target), gap and trend.

A chart illustrates the problem better than any written text

Expressing the problem by a chart has a huge impact; it can tell a lot more visually and is much more effective than a few lines of text. The run chart is a graphic way of quickly expressing the gap and the trend that the problem is having, including the distance from the goal and the severity of the situation. The run chart also allows you to highlight whether the problem is a caused problem or a created problem. This is a very important point, which is also helpful for guiding through the actions to be carried out in the later stages.

Caused Problems and Created Problems

The Caused Problems are problems that arise due to events that are out of control.

These problems occur when suddenly it is no longer possible to get the results that were obtained earlier. There is a decline in the ability to produce consistent results with those obtained in the past and the decay has already reached an insufficient performance level, so the situation is no longer acceptable and there is a gap.

The Created Problems however, occur when what we have always done in the past is no longer enough to meet today's expectations; it is no longer considered sufficient so we need to raise the bar of the targets.
There may be many factors that lead people and organisations to set new goals and to trigger an improvement process towards new goals. That's how new records are achieved in sports, how companies force the competitors to chase them, how new products and new projects are developed.

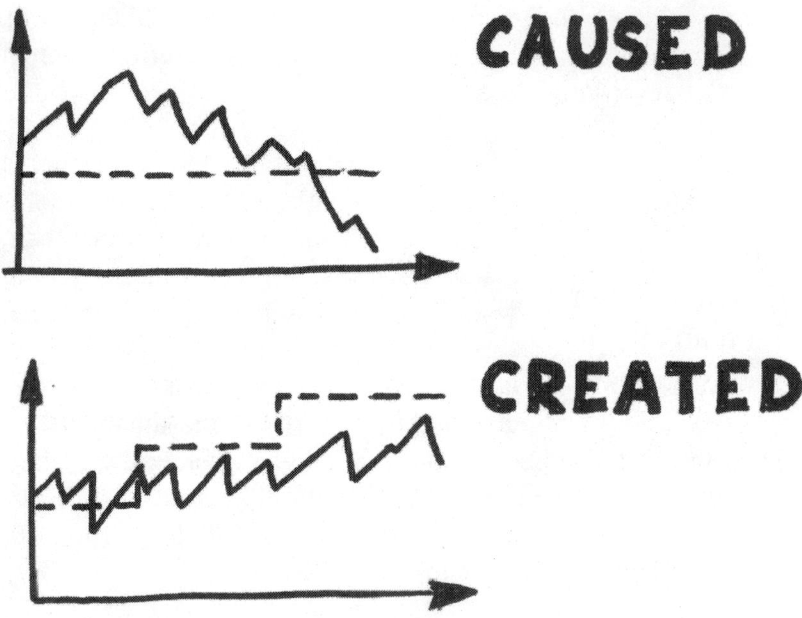

Fig: 3.3: Caused Problems and Created Problems

In Figure 3.3 we see in the first chart the example of an indicator that we would like to stay above the dotted line, which unfortunately is not happening in recent times, while in the second we would like also to remain above the dotted line, however periodically the target raises to higher levels which we have never been able to reach in the past.
The big differences between Caused Problems and Created

Problems reside:

1. in the sense of urgency to find solutions
2. in the directions in which to conduct the investigations

If the problem is Caused we need to go back to the time when the performance changed. In the run chart we do not have to look to the time when the actual line starts to cross the target line, we must identify when the actual line starts to deviate from the desired trend; that's the most important point in which to look for causes.

It is important to perform all the investigations by looking for what happened in the period -on the X axis- in which the trend changed, so that we can analyze the possible causes to mitigate or manage them appropriately.

Regarding instead the sense of urgency that normally accompanies the problems, when you deal with a Caused Problem you typically have little time, so the sense of urgency to fix the problem is very high: getting back to the performance levels of the processes involved in the problem is of vital importance, and the solution has to be found.

the sense of urgency is much higher in the Caused Problems

If we were able in the past to achieve certain results, the urgency is to understand why we cannot reach them anymore.

There are no more excuses, it is important not to lose time.

On the other hand, The Created Problems however can be solved with an additional dose of innovation and experimentation; for this reason the urgency to fix this type of problems is lower.

In these cases we have a certain period of time to explore new methods and tools in order to achieve new goals and we must also have time to stabilise the output on the new results achieved.

Moreover, dealing with a Created Problem with the aim to reach new performance and new levels of quality and service, doesn't run the risk of immediate loss of Customers and market share.

In addition to this, there is another big difference between the Caused Problems and Created Problems in terms of action plans: we will have typically fast countermeasures in a short-term plan in case of caused problems (remember the sense of urgency).

Differently, we will have sufficient time to issue an action plan having medium/long term actions in the second case. It is quite obvious when dealing with Created Problems as experimentations and innovations require more time to be evaluated and implemented.

Mixed Type Problems

Often the line between a Caused Problem and a Created Problem is not sharp. It happens more often than expected that a Created Problem can be treated like a mixed type Problem.

Most of the Created Problems actually fall under the mixed problems definition; we are asked to reach new performances and new levels of quality because the current goals are continuously stretched.

These are like the case of the high jump, in which the bar is raised even more to try to achieve better and better performances.

We are not asking the athlete to invent a new sport; we are asking him to further develop a skill that he already possesses, to improve his athletic form and his training program, to take care of his diet and his explosive strength in order to continue to do what he already know how to perform, the high jump, but with better results.

Thanks to this approach, in the history of the high jump we have seen the introduction of 4 different techniques that have enabled year by year to greatly improve the performances of the high jump athletes.

In the beginning of the XIX century Olympic Games the record was equal to 163 cm (5 ft. 4 in) and came to the considerable height of 245 cm (8 ft. 0¼ in) at the time of this writing, until someone else will manage to solve the (created) problem to exceed this height.

Imagine being asked to improve your elevation when you are the holder of the Olympic record of 163 cm (5 ft. 4 in). And imagine what might have been ridiculous to even speculate exceeding 200 cm (6 ft. 6¾ in).

Year	**Style**	**Athlete**	**High**
1895	*Scissors*	Michael F. Sweeney	1,97 m, 6 ft 5½ in
1912	*Western Roll*	George Horine	2,01 m, 6 ft 7 in
1978	*Straddle*	Vladimir Jaščenko	2,35 m, 7 ft 8 ½ in
1993	*Fosbury*	Javier Sotomayor	2,45 m 8 ft 0¼ in

Fig: 3.4: World Records using four different high jump techniques, from Wikipedia

The problem, a Created Problem, has been faced by athletes, those that were holding the records or those who were willing to beat the existing one, that have thought out of the box which ways were feasible to raise the known limit to a newer level.

They have not learned to fly, they just perfected and optimised the method by which they jump up, sometimes changing it as the table in Fig. 3.4 shows. In these terms, the problem is created, but is a mixed type, something to improve by using methods already known, sometimes introducing small changes to them.

This phase is furthermore facilitated by the creation of an open environment in your group of collaborators. It is possible that others may have ideas or stimulants and would be a waste not to put these people in a position to share their thoughts, giving a follow up, encouraging and rewarding those who propose new ideas. To succeed in this endeavor also means removing the so-called "eighth waste" of lean manufacturing, the unused creativity, a creativity practically free of charge.

An example of a created problem that has not been addressed as a mixed problem is the one solved with the birth of aviation, or the problem that led to the birth of the magnetic levitating train, examples of scenarios in which it was necessary to invent a new method, a new technology as the improvement of existing methods would have not permitted the achievement of new performances sufficient to fill a very large gap.
Not even flapping his arms very strong has man ever been able to fly autonomously. Not even flapping stronger and stronger (pointless for you to try, it never worked).

At least so far.

Given that the majority of created problems are of the mixed type, there are still not many excuses if the desired result is not achieved. Although motivated by a sense of less urgency, it is still possible to apply a continuous improvement logic to every skill and every feature or function.

This is easy enough to destroy the alibi of those who do not want to cooperate to solve a "created" problem as it is too difficult to solve. Every progress is triggered by the creation (conscious or unconscious) of problems.

Thanks to our tree model, measuring the problem through the four metrics (Actual, Goal, Gap and Trend) and the run chart, we can evaluate how far away we are from the standard we have defined. This situation is the ideal starting point to make some measurable progresses.

To understand and to measure the gap allows us to take all the necessary actions to reduce it to an acceptable value while maintaining full control of the situation, without the risk of over-or underestimate any stage of the problem solving process.

Over the following chapters we will address the steps of solving problems, relying on the fact that a careful definition of the problem is critical to properly proceeding towards its resolution, and that the problem definition, when well done, is already one-third of the work.

Page intentionally left blank

4. SEARCHING FOR THE CAUSES *(where)*

Goal

In order to effectively analyze what has sparked the problem, we need to understand where the analysis needs to be carried out. In this chapter we will analyze the methods to identify the correct place in which to conduct the investigations.

Content

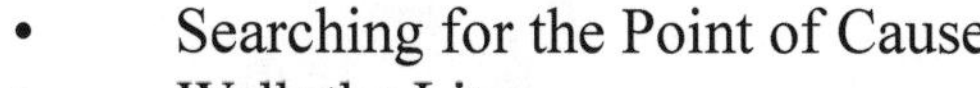

- Searching for the Point of Cause
- Walk the Line
- The Gemba, the Real Place
- The Senses of Man
- The Bulb Brainteaser
- Pie Charts
- The Business Case of the Small Parts
- The Various Types of Gemba

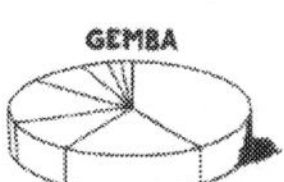

Fig: 4.1: The APS doughnut: Where

Searching for the Point of Cause

As we have seen, the definition phase of the problem is one of the key moments to solving the problem successfully.
As soon as the problem definition has been carried out we can move to the "where" phase that leads us to understand where is the place in which the problem has been caused, or where are the points of attack to solve a created problem.

Being able to figure out the "where" allows us to conduct the investigations in an efficient way. It also allows us to be effective in the analysis of the causes, an important condition to solve the problem.

> What happens in episodes of detective films or thrillers? Finding the dead man (the problem is having one man killed instead of zero, a measurable gap) does not mean we already have found the place where the murder took place; often the discovery of the murder victim is only a preamble

to the search of the crime scene, that does not necessarily coincide with the place in which the body is discovered; we are talking about primary and secondary crime scenes.

As long as we do not understand where the murder took place we have only identified the secondary scene of the crime. The primary scene of the crime is the one that contains answers to the questions of the investigators, answers that support the research of the murderer.

Moreover, without this research for the primary crime scene, the episodes of detective films would probably not last enough to comply with the movies or TV formats.

Walk the Line

To search for the point where the problem has been caused is an activity that in Toyota is defined as "Walk the Line", meaning walking backwards the flow of material, next to the production line.

The scenario is the following: there is a problem on the production line and a search in the opposite direction is immediately activated (going upstream in the production line is equivalent to moving from the crown to the roots of the tree in our model). But what are we looking for?

The aim is to search and find the point of the production line where the problem has occurred or could occur, knowing already that there is a point downstream in the production line (a most recent event in the timescale) which shows evidently that there is a problem.

The Gemba, the Real Place

Back to the primary crime scene, to the place where the cause has occurred, consists in searching for the "Gemba" (Westernisation of the Japanese word Genba, to be pronounced with a hard G: "gèm-ba").

Gemba means "the real place", the place in which the creation of value takes place. In our case it means where the causes of the problem are. The term "Go to Gemba" indicates the need to physically visit the place where the chances of finding out what happened are maximised. So what?

Go to Gemba!

Go to Gemba every time you can!!

In the detective series Gemba is the place where the murder took place, the murder of the individual whose body was later found somewhere else.

The police movies and books rely heavily on this formula to make big impressions on the viewers or readers and to prove that the cases can be solved brilliantly. Also the problems can be solved brilliantly and, like the police, it is the precise identification of the true Gemba that facilitates the task.

The possibility to identify the Gemba and to go to that place(s) allow us to make ballistic measurements, to discover boxes of ammunition, to search for cigarette butts on which to collect the DNA, to collect the recordings of CCTV cameras that frame the scene, to interview the potential witnesses, or, in general, to collect any other relevant information to reconstruct the events.

On top of this, there is another big advantage, the opportunity to use all our senses to reach a level of completeness of the investigation that a written report or a relief, by its nature, cannot convey to the inquirer.

Not to mention that most of the time the reports are not well done and the maker may not exactly know what to look for.

Have you ever read the reports made by the authorities intervened on the sidelines of a car accident?

The Gemba is the "real place", in which the value is added

A written report will never provide a full reconstruction of the incident as if you had been on the site in person. What can happen, however, if you go in person to the crash site?

You definitely would of understood more clearly how the facts may have happened, you would also have the opportunity to check environmental conditions, to use your senses, sight, smell, touch, taste, hearing, even proprioception, to collect as much data as is required about the possible causes, interferences or amplifications.

To be at Gemba, after having the problem well defined, allows us to have precise and specific questions to ask. Who carries a relief may not have our level of knowledge of the problem, may not have the same answers and therefore may not have the same hunger for information and probably, not at our level of determination.

The interactions with the environment does not end there: we can also view from different angles, interviewing people, use natural or artificial light sources, to deliberately prevent some of our senses from capturing information (ears or eyes can be isolated to gather more information) and finally to respond with greater completeness and success to the doubts that arise and to the questions that we have.

The same thing happens when novels are transformed into movies.

Those who read the novel have a personal understanding of the story, and suddenly, it is never the same story that is represented at the cinema, the one that has been perceived by the filmmakers. The film director tells the reality that he has understood by reading and analyzing the book, and that is able to reconstruct spectacularly, which inevitably is different by the other reconstructions made by anybody else.

How can a written report tell to all the readers the same reality?

Simple, it cannot.

In a situation where every viewer inevitably re-creates their own reality, the risk of making mistakes is very high. The condition that we need to recreate to analyze scenarios with success is, first, to understand where the Gemba is and then to physically "go to Gemba" to conduct investigations, to collect evidences and gather answers to our questions, whether existing or stimulated by what we are experiencing.

The Senses of Man

"Go to Gemba" becomes the password that allows us to continue with the investigation and finally solve the problem. It is us, not others, that should go to Gemba, whenever possible, to maximise the use of the twelve senses nature has provided us (according to the model of Rudolf Steiner):

The lower senses:

- Sense of life
- Sense of self-movement
- Sense of balance
- Sense of touch (Sense of the skin)

The middle senses:

- Sense of warmth
- Sense of taste
- Sense of smell
- Sense of sight

The upper or higher senses:

- Sense of hearing
- Sense of speech
- Sense of thought
- Sense of individuality

Although excluding the first and the last, which are objectively of little help during an investigation such as this, there are still ten ways that can allow us to gather much more information than a third party report.

The Bulb Brainteaser

A classic riddle can be used to highlight the effectiveness of the practice of going to Gemba.

Riddle:
"which switch controls the light bulb that is placed inside the box?"

Fig: 4.2: The brainteaser of the bulb and the three switches

The conditions are:

- The bulb is off at this moment.
- Only one switch, out of three, is wired to the bulb.
- You can operate the switches as many times you want, before opening the box.
- The box is completely dark and you cannot see from the

outside if the bulb is on or off, you can only assess it by removing the box cover.

- The box can be opened only once, and that is the moment in which you have to provide the correct answer, without having any other chances to operate the switches.
- The wiring doesn't provide any useful information about which switch is connected to the bulb.
- You must provide the answer being 100% sure which is the correct switch.

Give yourself a few minutes now to solve the riddle before discovering the solution in the next few pages of the book. Please acknowledge that you are not looking for a magicians trick, you are just willing to discover the correct sequence of actions that can give you a 100% correct solution.

Try it now...

Solved?

Normally team work facilitates the identification of the problem, and this is not only due to the fact that in a large group of people it is more likely that one of the members already know the solution. The team is able to create value much faster as long as all individuals feel free to speak out and give their own ideas in a sort of brainstorming (activities which will be described in Chapter 7, where we will discuss countermeasures).

When the team knows the importance of going to Gemba, the solution will not be long in coming.

Those who are familiar with the mathematics and statistics may say that you cannot solve a problem like this (three switches and only one chance to open the box to look at the bulb). The problem solver, however, knows that the extra edge is "go to gemba".

Where is the gemba in this riddle?

Which is the place where the creation of value happens? where can I go to answer the question?

The Gemba, in this riddle is the inside of the box, isn't it?
But the box can be opened only once, no more than once, and at that point you have to give the answer. If you think and imagine a light bulb, and analyze the function of the light bulb, if you analyse the reason why the bulb is installed, you can imagine that it can have two statuses: on and off.
This deduction is an asset but is not enough to answer with certainty the question "Which is the switch that controls the light bulb?".
However, if you go to gemba what can you find?

Opening the box to physically reach the Gemba, you can find that there are other answers that may be collected using all my senses. Try to stop reading for a moment and imagine how you might find the bulb with each of your senses….
Could smell something burning?
Could make a noise?
It might be rough, smooth, wet or dry?
It might be cold? Or hot?
It may move or be fixed?
And so on...

Here's what you can do: you can use all your senses to gather information and answer the original question: which of the three switch turns on the light bulb that was originally off, by going to gemba once? The problem solver, by going to Gemba, discovers new details; he understands which of the three switches controls the bulb through the use of the senses: the bulb can be either on, or off-and-cold, or off-and-warm.

Hence Gemba has given us new and valuable information to help in understanding what's behind a problem and helps us to build a piece of history that was not known at the beginning, that piece of history that contains the causes to our problem.

But how many Gemba are there?

The Gemba is not just one, everything can be Gemba, and it just depends on what we're looking for!

Let's start to take advantage of the initial investment, the fact that we have identified the correct way to measure the problem by a measurable gap. If what we are able to observe at Gemba is able to explain exhaustively the Gap, then the Gemba is only one, otherwise, if the explanations can only partially justify our problem, we must look for other Gemba that contain parts of the causes of the gap that are still not explained.

In other words, the identification of Gemba, the places where the creation of value actually happen (where our Gap as a whole is created, because for us understanding the Gap means gaining value), allows us to understand where are the roots of the tree that we are analyzing.
Later on, going to the places represented by the base of the tree, we can understand what are the main roots that support the tree as a whole. These roots, when cut or removed, will cause the death of the tree itself and all the symptoms that are related to it will disappear.
The problem will be solved.

The Pie Charts

The size of the roots (that represents how much each Gemba, if more than one, is worth in the problem) can be shown by a pie chart, a particular type of chart that illustrates very effectively the size of different areas, and allows to easily identify those most significant, those in which is worth going to analyze what may have happened.
For our purposes, the pie chart can be represented starting from 12 o'clock, going clockwise, to highlight the importance of each Gemba, in descending order.

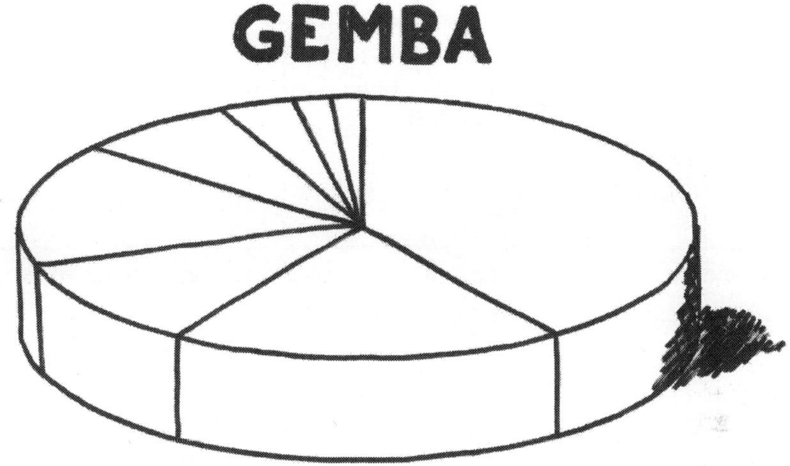

Fig: 4.3: The "Where" Pie Chart

In the upper right area we will have the greatest slice, the most interesting for our investigation, and we'll gradually find smaller and smaller slices moving clockwise on the cake.

To avoid wasting energy by going to those Gemba which have little importance and may contain few answers, we consider only the area of the chart that goes from midnight until 10 am (moving clockwise, the first three quarters of the pie) to cope with the strategy of physically visiting only the Gemba that most likely contain important answers to our inquiries.

In addition, this is also a cheap strategy as going physically to Gemba may also lead to real transportation, food and accommodation costs.

Sometimes, not always, going to Gemba may be inexpensive for two reasons: the first is that Gemba could be very close to reach without any charge, the second is because:

Gemba may not even be a physical place!

This interpretation of the meaning of Gemba is very important. Gemba is not necessarily a geographical area, a place where we need to go. Gemba can also be a period in the past in which to look for evidences, a type of instrument used, a phase of an operation, a person within a work group, a particular time of the day, a language, a different type of lighting and also a mix of environmental conditions.

Gemba is not necessarily a physical place

Gemba may be any element of diversity that allows us to isolate an area on which to focus our investigation.

The Business Case of the Small Parts

Let's try to understand better the effectiveness and meaning of Gemba through the analysis of this problem (actually happening for real):
A company that produces small pieces, made by metal and rubber, has an agreement with a distributor overseas to deliver in bulk (without final packaging) large quantities of small parts which will be later packaged by the local distributor. The pieces are packed in vacuum bags to prevent the parts from moving and scratching each other. In this case the parts may become dirty, especially when the white part of a rubbcry piccc touchcs thc mctal part of anothcr piccc, smcaring and staining of metal oxide.

The vacuum bag is a transparent bag through which the final visual inspection of the pieces can be done and this allows the showing of photographs that the pieces on consignment are leaving the company in perfect condition.

But what happens is that the distributor complains regularly saying that the pieces that he receives are so dirty and unusable.

Additional checks on the goods leaving the warehouse of finished products reveal that the pieces sent to wholesale customers are of excellent quality, they are perfectly vacuum-packed and therefore they do not move during transport at the point to get dirty.

An additional test is performed by carrying here and there for a few days the bags with few cars, simulating the vibrations that may occur.

This test is used to confirm that the pieces do not get dirty and remain perfect even after several hours of travel, confirming that the packaging method is suitable for the purpose.

In the meantime the supplier begins to believe it is the wholesaler that does not correctly handle the pieces and eventually deteriorates them by opening the vacuum bag without making proper attention during the packing stage.
Meanwhile, complaints and returns continue to arrive even on subsequent deliveries, so that the commercial partnership is at risk.

A group of Problem Solvers is therefore involved in this problem which is supposed to depend on the poor ethics of the distributor. The group begins to work and simply collect objective information without endorsing at first the ethics, to reach the stage at which they have to figure out which is the real Gemba that can provide answers to the analysis of possible causes.

They start with the analysis of the pictures made by the customer on the bags received and still under vacuum, pointing out that some parts arrive dirty to the distributor. There was doubt whether the bag could have been opened and closed; however, on the pictures it appeared still intact with the packaging seals. After this, however, the investigation has been to understand what is the pathway the pieces follows after leaving the finished goods inventory of the production site up to being received in the warehouse of the distributor overseas.

The path is then analyzed, it consists of the following steps: Transporter (truck), central repository, automated sorting on belts, airport cargo to the aircraft, flight, unload from the aircraft at destination, automatic sorting, manual handling, road transport, delivery to the destination.

The challenge is to identify which of these steps have different characteristics from the vibration tests performed previously, to identify which step constitutes the true Gemba, that Gemba must give explanations that the vibration test is not able to give, and thanks to this analysis it turns out that there is a big difference all right: it is the air travel, lasting several hours on a modified atmospheric pressure, as occurs at high altitude in a cargo hold.

In these conditions the bag enters the aircraft perfectly vacuum sealed, it is unloaded at the destination perfectly vacuum sealed, but during the flight tends to swell slightly due to the lower difference of air pressure between the inside and the outside of the bag (in high altitude the atmospheric pressure which presses the outside of the bag is more bland).

This creates the conditions so that the pieces can move between each other due to vibration of the aircraft. The identification of the real Gemba could provide a credible explanation of what is going on to cause the problem.

At the supplier's site it was decided, therefore, that the creation of the vacuum is not sufficient, and that the solution could have been found applying a pressure from the outside on the bag layers, to avoid the conditions of lower atmospheric pressure during flight at high altitude could trigger the movements of the small parts.

A new packaging in corrugated cardboard has been tested, with sheets of foam to compress each of the small parts within the bag, using the solid backing of the inner walls of the box and relying on the elasticity of the structure of the foam.

The foam continues to perform the same pressure on the small parts, regardless of the external pressure. This allowed the pack to reach the destination without allowing reciprocal movement between the parts.

The small pieces stopped getting dirty.

The Different Types of Gemba

As previously indicated, Gemba is not necessarily in a physical place; let's see briefly where it may consist.

Examples of Gemba:

- a region, city, street or geographical location (e.g. the discovery of the dead man in the detective film or the low sales in certain regions)
- a period in the past or a recurring cycle (think about the sales performance of seasonal products)
- the type of instrument used (transportation vehicle, tool, measuring device)
- a component of equipment that performs a given function
- a person in a group, which has the characteristics we are looking for
- a tool out of our toolbox
- a system we use
- a working method we have adopted
- a phase of a work process
- an office, a department or a workgroup in an organisation
- an ingredient in our recipe

- a language not understandable or unsuitable
- a specific sports opponent (we always lose against that team)

... and many many more.

5. WHY DO WE HAVE THE PROBLEM? *(why)*

Goal

Thanks to the identification of the real Gemba, it is now possible to obtain the maximum effectiveness from the analysis of the causes of our problem.
Correctly identifying the main reasons is the key to go straight to the point to fix.

Content

- The Main Causes
- The Root Causes
- The Pareto Law
- Pie & Why
- The Vital Few

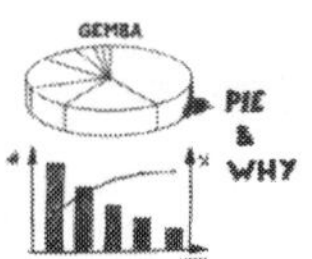

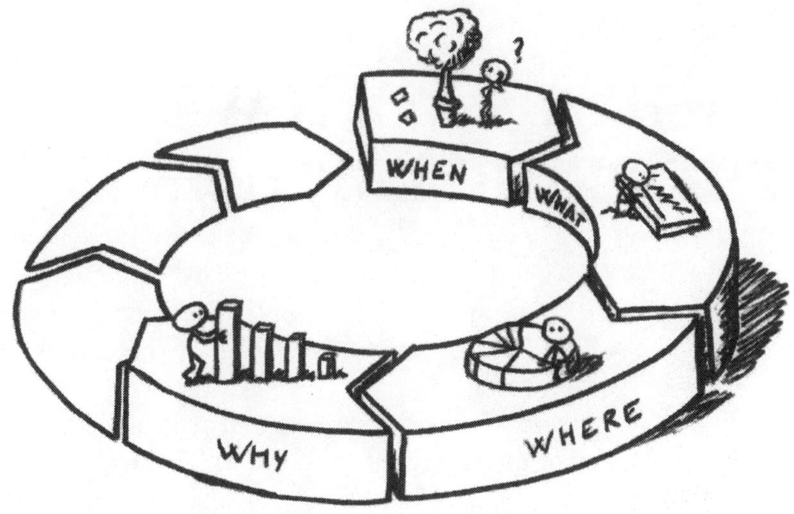

Fig: 5.1: The APS Doughnut: Why

The Main Causes

The answers collected at Gemba, physically visiting the sites that contain the answers to our questions, must be used to proceed with the next step. After being identified, Gemba is the significant place in which to answer the questions "Why did it happen?"

Probably the most obvious "because" it has already been identified and corresponds to the roots of our biggest tree, but it has the disadvantage to answer the question "why did it happen?" only superficially.
The fact that they are so clear to be evident in the very first reconstruction of the history of the tree means that they are superficial and insufficient to solving the problem. Indeed, despite being known causes, they do not allow us to find solutions to the problem so far.

How can we proceed to investigate the reasons behind these visible causes, these apparent causes, in order to identify the real Root Cause that needs to be fixed?

The Root Causes

We must first clarify what the Root Causes are. They are the deepest causes of the problems, responsible for the problematic situation. Only by identifying and stating the problem correctly, also only identifying the meaningful Gemba(s), and only conducting the investigation properly, the deepest causes can then be identified. They are the root causes, the ones from which originate the roots that continue to provide nourishment to the tree.

Thanks to them, the tree continues to live and to germinate, even if you cut a branch or if a small root is cut away.
In other words, focusing on the main roots from which the tree draws its nourishment corresponds to a new 80/20 approach to work only on those few causes that feed most of the problem.
From these roots it is therefore desirable to search and analyze the deeper causes, deep down to the root causes. It is like digging down with a paddle, following the path of the bigger roots under the ground, to understand how deep they go and gaining a new perspective and understanding of the complexity of the roots themselves.

As well as in the analogy of the tree, the root causes of our problems are not visible without digging down in the ground, without analyzing and understanding in depth which are the biggest ones. This approach is helpful as it avoids wasting time and resources with smaller and not so useful roots, working only on those that support the tree.
Digging is hard, so you should understand what are the most important roots to bring to light.

The Pareto's Law

The histogram of Pareto is a great method to graphically represent the impact of the so-called "vital few", which are nothing more than the few causes accountable for most part of the problem, in a relationship that has been shown to be frequently in the percentage of 80% - 20%.

Vilfredo Pareto, an economist who lived between the years 1848 and 1923, studied the demographic correlations with wealth and found that the ratio 80/20 is recurrent in many situations. 80 percent of the wealth, in his studies, was in the hands of 20% of the population.
Later it was discovered that this proportion is recurrent in many other situations, so that you can use it to simplify complex situations, choosing to work on a few elements that are actually the most important.

In business it is quite common to discover, for example, that 80% of revenue comes from 20% of the articles or services, that 80% of the shares are held by 20% of the subjects, 80% of the problems derive from 20% of the causes and finally, every problem is solvable at least by 80% identifying and removing only 20% of the causes.

Fig: 5.2: A Pareto Histogram having a secondary Y axis

The histogram is built up as follows:

1. Identify the weight of each cause, expressed in the same units as the Gap (if the Gap is 10 and a primary cause responsible for two-thirds of it, its weight will be 6.6, and the same applies to all the causes)
2. Reorder the causes from the largest to the smallest

3. Draw on the histogram the bars showing from left to right the largest to the smallest, representing the most important causes by their weights on the left side (the weight is measured on the Y axis on the left)
4. To facilitate the identification of 80% at which to stop, we draw a line, referring to the Y axis to the right (secondary axis)
5. the values followed by the line are the cumulative percentage covered the bars the more we go from left to right. (Eg: the first cause explains 66% of the problem, if I add the second I go to 81%, with the addition of the third go to 87% and so on until the last which will cover 100% of the problem).

This rule is a great opportunity for the problem solver. From the point of view that labour economics is important to know that with 20% of the effort we can get 80% of the results, it is a huge opportunity not to be wasted.
Moreover, by dealing with the problems we inevitably face the complex reality, a method that requires simplification is a very big help to stay focused on the target in the easiest way.

Pie & Why

Do you remember? By identifying the Gemba with the pie chart we made a simplification, considering only the few most significant Gemba. Now we can exploit the new opportunities by focusing our efforts on the few elements that matter, the few "whys" that deserve to be investigated.

The "why" that falls under the Pareto 80/20 Rule are the main roots of the tree, the roots without which the tree itself would not be able to receive nourishment, without which it could not survive and would be destined to dry up and die.
Since we do not have time to dig for every single root, our effort must be in understanding where the main roots go, knowing that it will be sufficient to attack the roots to kill the tree and, with this, to kill the problem forever.

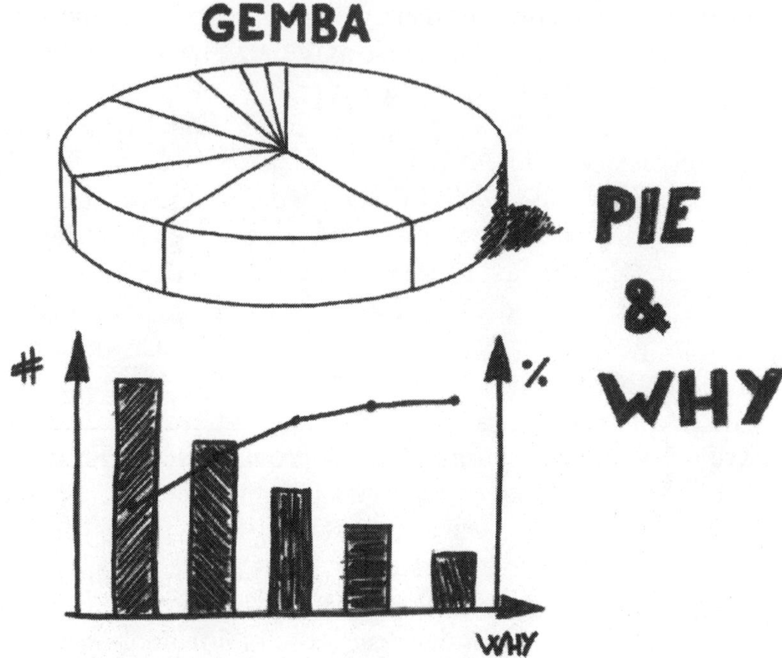

Fig: 5.3: Where and Why charts: the “Pie & Why” of APS

Once a few "whys" that support the trunk of the problem are identified, it is necessary to carry out the survey itself, performing the analysis directly by "going to Gemba" to be extraordinarily effective.

This is the phase in which the use of all the human senses, from each participant, will allow us to collect the maximum amount of information. By doing so, we can apply a very practical investigation by following the method of the five whys, which we will look into more depth in the next chapter. This method will allow us to identify the Root Causes of our problem.

The Vital Few

Before going on it is worth analyzing one aspect of this simplification: how can just 80% of Gemba, in which we will work only on 80% of the causes, let us close the gap to 100%?

We may mathematically be able to close just 64% of the gap, since we're considering only the eighty percent of the eighty percent of our problem (0, 8*0, 8 = 0, 64). But it's not.

Normally the original gap is closed because what constitutes as the original Gap is actually the difference between a situation that has changed from "acceptable" to "no longer acceptable". The starting point was not a perfect situation. For this reason, when we decide to work on a Gap, often we do not get back to the starting situation which was only "acceptable" (and therefore imperfect), but working on it, we are normally able to improve it further, overachieving the expected result. This is why it is sufficient to work on few vital elements to close the gap completely and, sometimes, also going beyond.

Page intentionally left blank

6. THE RESPONSIBLE PROCESS *(which)*

Goal

Thoroughly analyze the causes to identify the root cause responsible for the problem. This is a crucial stage to be able to apply the solutions.

Content

- The Five Why's
- The Collection of Information
- The Paths of Investigation
- Repeat the Investigation Avoiding Claims
- Rule # 1: Not Guilty
- Rule # 2: Units of Measure
- Money as an Excuse
- Rule # 3: The MIN Process
- The KSF, Key Success Factors
- The Final Checks

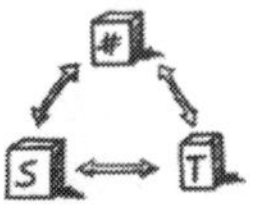

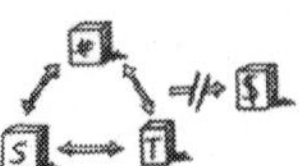

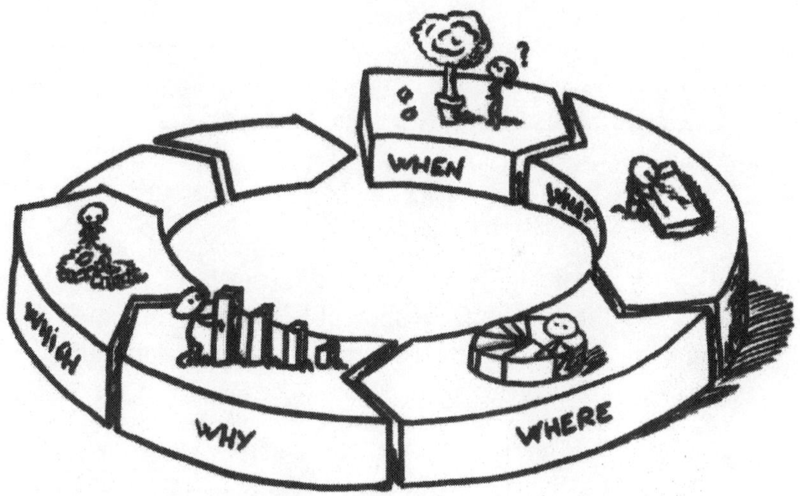

Fig: 6.1: The APS Doughnut: Which

One of the most important elements of Applied Problem Solving is discussed in this chapter. This element is of fundamental importance although of disarming simplicity, we say that it is one of the true "discoveries" that the APS method will reveal to us. This will enable us to simplify the complex reality, gaining effectiveness in our remove-the-problem activities.

The Five Why's

We have identified which are the main "Gemba" where we need to focus our research for answers which means we have identified the main roots of the tree. Well, we are now equipped to carry out the analysis of the evidences collected at gemba, in order to investigate the original cause at the base of the roots.

As mentioned in the previous chapter, one of the most popular methods is the 5 why's approach.

This method is, once again, a simplified approach to the management of complex realities; it consists of asking "why" a few times, not necessarily 5 times, to discover the relationships between cause and effect that reside along each of the roots of our tree, each of the 20% of the roots that provides support and nourishment to 80% of the tree.

The Collection of Information

The approach, besides being simple, is also very practical as it supposes that identification of causes and effects is carried out directly at Gemba, in that place where the answers already lie and we can find supportive evidences.

The collection of evidences at Gemba can be done thanks to:

- instrumental findings
- interviews
- video shoots
- verification of KPI's[12]
- photos/pictures
- collection of samples to be analyzed
- perception of the environment as a whole
- evaluation of the climate of collaboration
- testimonials
- acquisition of any CCTV recordings

.. and many more.

The very effective approach is to physically go to Gemba to perform the analysis which can be directly carried out by using all our senses. This enables us to perceive in a broader way the situation and keep us far away from collecting prejudicial information.

---

[12] The KPIs are also known as Key Performance Indicators. They are the visible part of a deeper philosophy of control and management of processes using the Visual Management dictates. This method involves the identification and the use of given indicators (charts, tables, visual signals) directly at Gemba to publish some of the operating parameters of the process that are carried out in that workspace. For example, the speedometer is a method of displaying one of the parameters to run effectively and safely a car.

At Gemba, the collection of information should be performed in small steps, taking care to maintain consistency between each step and avoiding falling off the road, while looking for the root causes.

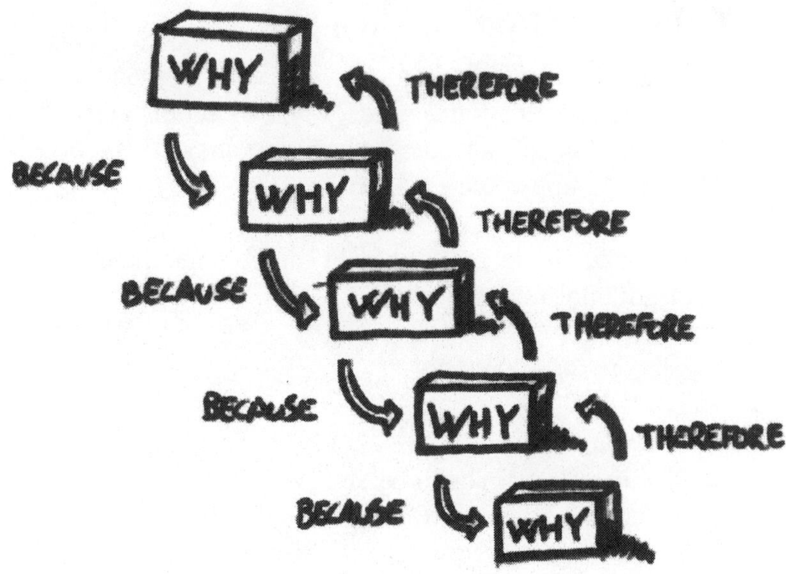

Fig: 6.2: The five why's method

The answer to the first why, the one at the trunk of our tree, will become a new why, a new question which will provide a further response to go even deeper. This is the activity that, digging deeper and deeper, allows the root of the tree to get fully discovered, exposing the deeper parts of each root and showing where it goes.

The deepest point reached by the root is identified as the Root Cause that we need to eliminate.

The Paths of Investigation

A typical 5 why's path may be the following one:

The car doesn't start.

- Why can the car not be started?

→ because the battery is low.

- Why is the battery low?

→ Because I left the lights on when I parked.

- Why have the lights been left on?

→ Because I was not paying attention and I have not noticed they were still on.

- Why didn't you notice they were still on?

→ Because the lights don’t switch off by removing the keys and the car doesn’t provide any advice.

It is evident from this example that if the lights are switched off automatically by the car or the equipment included an acoustic signal for the user, the likelihood of having the car unable to start due to low battery will significantly reduce. This is something that already happens in all newer cars.

Let us look at a different example, related to the safety in the workplace:
→ The operator of the milling machine had their fingernail ripped out, getting very close to losing the finger.

- Why did this near miss happen?

→ because he was operating the milling machine without wearing the safety gloves.

- Why wasn't he wearing the gloves?

→ because the use of gloves reduces sensitivity to what he is doing.

- Why does he need sensitivity?

→ because he must handle small parts that require high

sensitivity.

It seems clear that, in this investigation, the research for the root cause is more complex.
However, we must learn to realise that this survey was not conducted in an appropriate manner, so that the point where we get to is not a root cause and is not manageable; so are we concluding that it is impossible to safely handle small parts processed through a milling machine?

Is it useful to have a survey conducted in this way?

Repeat the Investigation Avoiding Claims

This lack of investigation is immediately realised by any expert problem solver. Moreover, we can also identify the reason why the investigation is wrong (if is the case) and we can then repeat it the correct way, highlighting a manageable root cause. In the last example it seems that the solution is to stop handling small pieces, or to do it without sensitivity wearing the gloves; these two things severely limit the ability to resolve the problem quickly and economically. Let's perform the investigation in a different way:

→ The operator of the milling machine had their fingernail ripped out, getting very close to losing the finger.

- Why did this ncar miss happcn?

→ because he operated on the milling machine without paying enough attention.

- Why didn't he pay enough attention?

→ because he was distracted.

- Why was he distracted?

→ because he had not been sufficiently trained in that type of activity and the risks that entails.

Does this look more familiar?
Even if it does, this doesn't mean it is an effective investigation.

This survey seems to be more easily resolvable because it brings to light a lack of training, so in a timely manner and with little cost, we can proceed with the instruction of the operators to ensure that they will operate safely in the future.

Sooner or later, though, someone else will get hurt, or will run the risk of getting hurt.

This will happen because the new 5 why's investigation has shifted the causes to the operator, accusing him of working distractedly and/or without training. The approach attributes the deficiency exclusively to the operator; this focus is not sufficient to ensure that nobody else will get hurt again in the future. In the future other people might get close to moving parts of the machine with their hands, deliberately or carelessly, or even for an illness or fainting.
For these reasons the solution cannot rely solely on the level of attention the operator can maintain for the entire working day, otherwise there's a risk of going back home with one less finger.

Let's make the investigation once more, being careful not to accuse anyone of making mistakes and avoiding inconsistency as already happened in the first case we've seen:

→ The operator of the milling machine had their fingernail ripped out, getting very close to losing the finger.

- Why did this near miss happen?

→ because he could get close to the moving parts of the machine with his hand.

- Why could he put his hand in such a dangerous area?

→ because the moving parts are free to be reached by the operator's hand.

- Why are the moving parts free to be reached by the operator's hand?

→ because there is no system in place to ensure that the operators cannot reach the moving parts of the machine with their hands.

By setting up the investigation this way it seems even trivial as it highlights the true deficiency. Moreover this make easier to fix the root cause which, once removed, ensures the non-repeatability of the problem. In other words, concluding that the cause is the distracted operator and avoiding a new distraction happening again in the future is impossible to ensure.
In parallel, justifying the misuse of personal protection equipment such as gloves to handle the small pieces is minor and does not lead to a manageable cause, so it does not help to solve the problem.

On the other hand, to effectively conduct the 5 why's investigation helps to understand in an almost trivial way what are the root causes of the problem.

Let's move on to understand how we can conduct simple but effective investigations.

The rules to keep in mind are 3. Let's see.

Rule # 1: Not Guilty

As first thing we need to avoid falling into the easy temptation to consider the human error as a cause on which nothing can be done. The human error is and will always be possible, we need to understand how to avoid human errors that lead to harmful consequences, or at least those kinds of consequences that continue to fuel the problem.
To conclude that the causes are the distractions, lack of training, utilisation or involvement of alternative staff, differences in language or culture does not help to solve the problem: there will always be a risk that in the future other distractions, other training deficiencies, other staff, other languages or cultures co-

exist with the problem.

We must understand how to deal with the investigation without eventually jumping to the easy conclusion of blaming someone. The only thing that we can easily get, but unfortunately is useless, is the identification of an easy excuse. It is not about blaming others that problems are solved.

Rule # 2: Units of Measure

The units of measure that guide the investigation for the 5 why's are surprisingly few, just four.
The first three we consider are occurrences, time and space. Moreover, the first two are the most frequent, which further simplifies the investigation activity.

Fig: 6.3: The unit of measure of the investigation

During the five why's investigation we have to identify which unit of measure of the three is the one that primarily guides the investigation. Changing units of measure during the investigation may be necessary but is an activity which is worth considering carefully, in order to avoid going astray or losing the link between cause and effect, and between the different why's.

Switching from occurrences to time means to think of a

frequency. Switching from occurrences to space means to think of a capacity (area or volume). Switching from time to space means to think of speed. For these reasons, the three units are depicted in a triangle and are connected to each other.

Fig: 6.4: the connections between units of measure

The fourth unit, the one we are not allowed to use, is money. The prohibition of jumping from one of the three to the fourth is a very strong statement that normally doesn't find people in tune with, but it is needed to help problem solvers in developing a mechanism of thought that opens the door to find a solution rather than settle for an excuse.

This empowers also the lateral thinking which is sometimes mentioned in the problem solving approach.

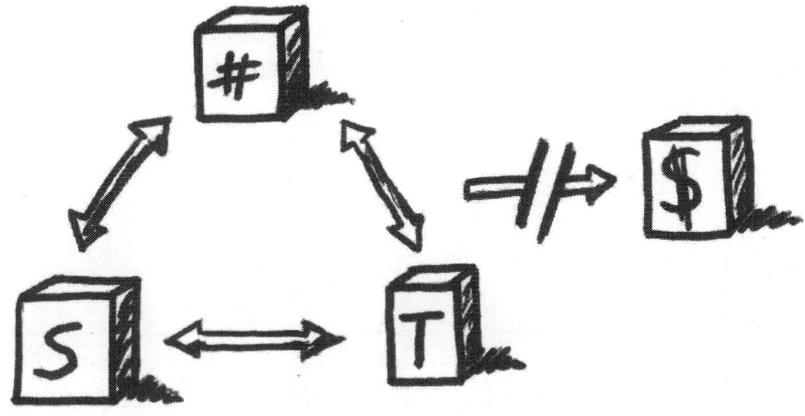

Fig: 6.5: jumping to money normally doesn't help to find an effective root cause

Money as an Excuse

If it was possible to shortcut to the money, for example, we would allow the conclusion that it is normal to drain the battery of a cheap car.
Should we have an expensive car it wouldn't have happened? It's normal to think that whoever got hurt it was due to the cheap milling machine; let's provide us a brand new expensive milling machine and very high skilled workers so we will be sure the fingers will stay in place.

Maybe.

Unfortunately it's not so simple, this does not happen for two reasons: the first is that the formula "infinite money" = "zero problems" is absolutely false.

We can add people in an office poorly organised but what we will get is more confusion; we can buy the most expensive car without achieving the goal of never having any fault; we can buy the most expensive equipment without having the guarantee that the parts will be machined correctly.
Spending more and more doesn't guarantee that we will have

the problem solved. Statistics often show that the best solutions have costs in the range of a few hundred dollars. Anyway, let's push ourselves into the identification of the root cause; we will discuss the solutions later on.

the formula "infinite money" = "zero problems" is absolutely false

There is another aspect that must be considered when, apparently, it seems appropriate to consider the money in our analysis for researching the root cause. We need to solve the problem, so that we got to this point having had rationale[13], we also have chosen not to dismiss the problem as it deserves priority, it would be a shame to give up right now as a result of a wrong analysis leading to the excuse of Money.

Following this wrong approach we would find ourselves looking for a loan instead of looking to which problem has to be fixed as we don't have the resources to fix all. The prioritisation should be driven by the severity of each problem, not by the cost of each solution.
We have to stay away from the danger of money excuses when we look for the root causes.

In conclusion we may add that, if the context of the problem is the workplace, asking for cash to solve problems does not guarantee the success of the initiative. Especially if your boss or sponsor is a problem solver as well and knows the rule.

Even the request to add more people to your workgroup is a solution that misleads the investigation towards the limited availability of money. What often happens is that, in the absence of stable and robust processes, the more people we add to a workgroup in a not-well structured environment the more confusion we create, without improving productivity. For this

13 Let's begin to use the term "rationale" which means, among other definitions, "which meets the criteria of functionality". In the quotations in this book, the term rationale is used as a noun to indicate someone who has "non-irrational" reasons to spend his time on the given problem.

reason, once again, the solution does not lie in the use of extra money to hire new people, but in the use of available and trained intelligence to figure out which part of the existing workflow is an obstacle to achieve the desired productivity.

So is it absolutely forbidden to use the money as a unit of measure?
No, it is not absolutely forbidden.

We can use it only in two cases:
1. The unit of measurement of the first "why" is expressed in money.
2. We find ourselves using the money during the investigation, not as an excuse but as a fundamental element in our analysis (here we have to be careful not to lie to ourselves).

The first case is the typical situation in which the issue has already been expressed in a currency like the Dollar, the Pound, the Euro, etc. as it could be if the problem is an economic gap that corresponds to the money that I had to save, earn or pay.
The second case is exactly the case that I'm stressing you not to use, the case in which we start from occurrences, time or space, but at a certain point in the investigation we find ourselves forced into jumping to money issues. The prohibition that I have placed in such specific cases can be transgressed, but we must know in that case the analysis has to be really solid and critics-proof, otherwise easy and probable disputes will not lead to anything.

I'm not going to give you examples of Time, Space or Occurrence Gaps that may have Money related root causes. The reason for this is that normally the experts in this field are you guys, and usually it's not a long wait to prove it.
I normally limit myself to breaking up this belief when I am face to face with an investigation which has been completed this way. It is much more effective to prove it on real cases instead of spending a lot of words in explaining theories.
By taking this approach is very easy for me to break down any

wrong investigation and quickly show my teammates that this is a difficult path that should have not been chosen.

Please remember, it is not about asking for more money that we will solve the problems. I am already convinced and I'm becoming convinced even more if I think of how easy is to put in doubt almost all the investigations being lead in this direction.

Rule # 3: The MIN Process

This rule is a crucial point of the whole Applied Problem-Solving methodology. Should I point out one of the most important paragraph of the entire book, I would definitely choose this one.

What is this rule about?

The concept is very simple: at the end of the five why's investigation, always, and when I mean always I mean A-L-W-A-Y-S, there is a MIN process, which a process that, digging at the deepest level of our roots, proves to be Missing, Incomplete or Not followed.

The process identified by the MIN acronym is the true root cause, it is the process responsible for what is happening.
One of the Root Causes of our problem has been identified.

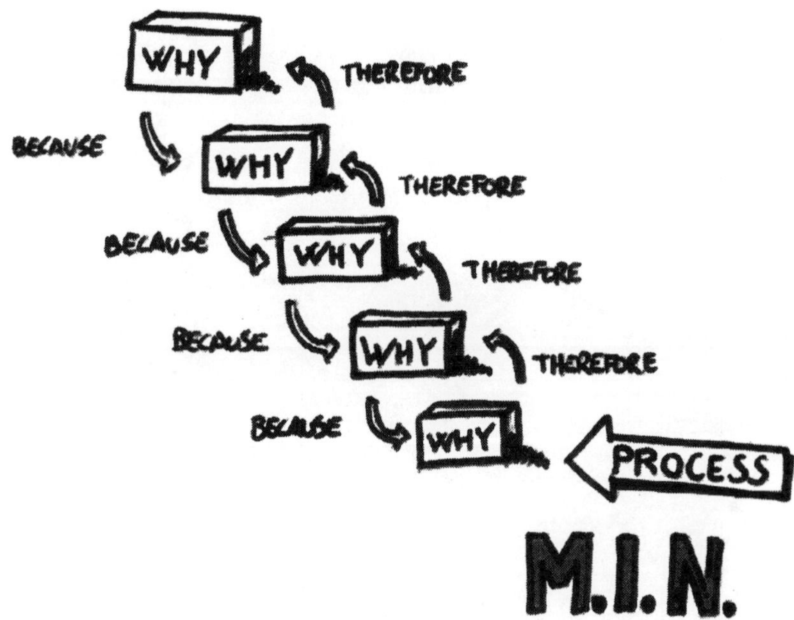

Fig: 6.6: The Root Cause is always a MIN process

The Root Cause is always a MIN process

It's very important to deeply acknowledge this concept. All those who are conducting investigations looking for the root causes, without keeping clear this in mind, are at risk of error.

The KSF, Key Success Factors

A brief digression from our method may serve to emphasise the importance of having stable and effective processes. In the Operations' world, there are well-defined concepts and methodologies that are being studied by APICS[14] which clearly and schematically define the key

[14] APICS: the Association for Operations Management ®, is an international non-profit educational organisation that offers certification programs, training tools, and a network of opportunities to increase professional performance.

factors for the success of organisations, called KSF (Key Success Factors). The KSF are also known as "Get It Right Factors", factors of doing things right, and represent everything that an organisation must do correctly to succeed in the competition. Should we be able to positively impact the KSF then we are on the right path.

The KSF are:
- Attributes of Products or Services
- Processes
- Costs
- Resources
- Capability

If we think about the use of our APS methodology, how many KSF can we positively impact?
The ability to highlight the MIN processes, which needs to be improved, satisfies the "Processes" KSF.
But what about the others KSF?

Let's look at the "costs" KSF; to have effective, stable and repeatable processes is the basis for improving themselves to a more efficient and profitable level, with high yield and low-waste. This translates into lower costs.
Let's look now at the "Resources" KSF: thinking of human resources, we can easily argue that people with good basic training and structured working methodologies, including APS, can certainly contribute to the success of organisations.

The "capability" KSF, instead, can be increased with a method that allows us to fill the gaps and to gain in efficiency.
Finally we can analyze the “attributes of the products or services”. This KSF is positively impacted by a structured methodology for problem solving, to exceed Customer's expectations; every time there is a "performance gap" (a failure from the point of view of functionality) we can

make it measurable so we will be able to analyze and solve it with APS.

If we return to the examples of the "five whys", shown earlier in the investigations, we see that the most effective are those that meet the three rules we've just described (not guilty, unit of measures and MIN process).

The case of the drawn battery in the car shows that the fault is not on those who buy and drive cheap cars, and it is not a money problem nor a problem related to the type of car. The problem stems from the fact that a process to ensure no errors are done is not effective, does not exist or is not followed by the users.

We can say that, in other words, an effective process to ensure nobody forgets the lights switch is on, is Missing, Incomplete or not followed.

- Not Followed:
    - Does the user manual somewhere mention the fact that leaving the lights on for too long without running the engine drain the battery?
    - Is the warning sound present and for unknown reasons the driver heard it but did not turn out the lights?
- Incomplete:
    - Is the warning sound activated with the opening of the door of the driver but for some reason the driver has dropped himself out from the opposite side?
    - Is the warning only activated by removing the keys from the ignition, but for some reason the keys were left plugged in?
    - Is the warning sound installed, but the automatism to turn off lights is absent?
- Missing:
    - Is there a system that alerts the driver and

automatically turns off the lights?

In all three cases, while thinking of different causes, it is always a process that has failed. If there had been an effective process the problem would not have occurred.
In the other five why's example that we studied, the one about the cut finger, the first investigation ended up with the failure in using gloves, it pointed out that a process existed but was not followed and insisted that it was impossible to follow the process because of sensitivity that was needed to handle small pieces. This was a process which, in some ways was also incomplete.

The second investigation failed miserably because attributed the blame to the operator for being distracted and was trying to find a solution in the education and training, a solution that by no means does not guarantee and cannot guarantee the elimination of the problem permanently.
The third investigation put out that the milling machine had no process in place to ensure that it is possible to safely move hands close to the moving parts. This is the best analysis as it highlights the lack of a process to prevent the accident, even in the case of distraction.
Should we identify exactly whether the process is an M, I or N type it doesn't matter, identifying the process is the foundation to find effective solutions.

The Final Checks

A trick that should always be used in any investigation conducted by the 5 whys method, is to carry out tests at each step, in order to verify that the path we are following continues to be consistent. These tests shall be to verify that all of the underlying layers satisfy completely the above why.

Let's see what it means to perform this test with the first example of the dead battery in the car:

The car doesn't start.

- Why can the car not be started?

→ because the battery is dead!

Before going on with the second "why" it is good to test our backlinks; in this case it's good to ask: "so if the battery was not dead then would it be possible to start the car?"
If the answer is "yes" without any doubt, then you can continue as the investigation is proven to be consistent.

Let's continue with "the battery is dead"...

- Why is the battery low (why it has run down)?

→ because I left the lights on when I parked

Check: so if I wouldn't have forgotten the lights were on then the battery should not have been drained?
Also in this case an affirmative answer, without doubt, confirms the validity of the analysis.

Let's continue with "I left the lights on when I parked"

- Why did I leave the lights on while parked?

→ because I was distracted and I did not notice.

So if I was not distracted I would have remembered to switch off the lights? Yes, it is true and it is the connected cause, so we can continue emphasising the process involved, not the fact that I was distracted....

- Why (since I was distracted) have I not noticed?

→ because if I park the car without switching the lights off the car does not report it and doesn't switch them off by its own.

So, should the car had been provided with an effective process to avoid forgetting the lights are on when parked, I would have noticed it even if distracted by other thoughts?
That's right, the distraction would have been managed in this

case.

A final check of the analysis carried out can be finally made by relating the last "because" with the first "why", to check whether the consistency is maintained:
"If a process had effectively managed the scenario where we can forget the lights are on when parked, it would have been possible to normally start the car."
That's true; the analysis has been well done.

Does it seem too simple? How comes that an easy solution is not implemented on 100% of cars on the roads?
Rather, it is likely that these connections look really simple because we're starting to think with the mind of the problem solver.
It's useful to note that there are cases where, in the "5 whys investigation", the question "why" can be answered with two or more complementary answers, which sum of the effects being exhaustively explained in the upper "why".
On the practical side this means that since one answer is not able to exhaustively respond to the above "why", therefore it is necessary to answer with two or more "because" statements at the lower level.
For each one of these peer-answers, the investigation branches into more investigations, each of them have to be developed and investigated on its own until the end (reaching the MIN process underneath).

This type of assessment for completeness takes advantage of the same concepts expressed by the MECE rule described in the hypotheses tree chapter. Remember that each answer when there is a branch must be MECE, mutually exclusive with respect to other branches that start from the same point and Collectively Exhaustive along with the other branches in order to represent 100% of the causes underlying the branch itself.
This is valid both for branches that depart from the trunk of the tree, and for those who find themselves in the "drill-down" activity carried out by the five whys method.

7. THE COUNTERMEASURES *(how)*

Goal

To analyze the techniques aimed to identify the countermeasures that, when applied, prevent the problem from reoccurring.

Content

- The Countermeasures
- Permanent Countermeasures
- Temporary Countermeasures
- Normalisations
- CSM Crawford Slip Method
- Classic Brainstorming
- The Opportunity Matrix
- Do, Plan, Evaluate, Forget
- To Make Things Happen

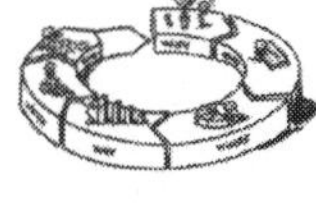
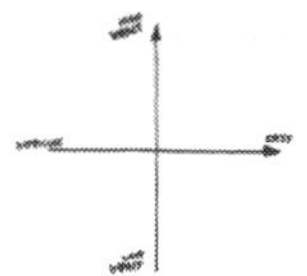
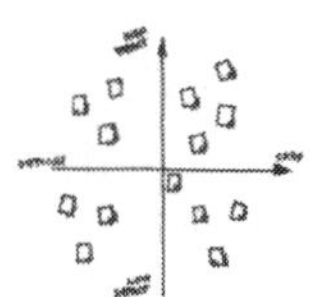

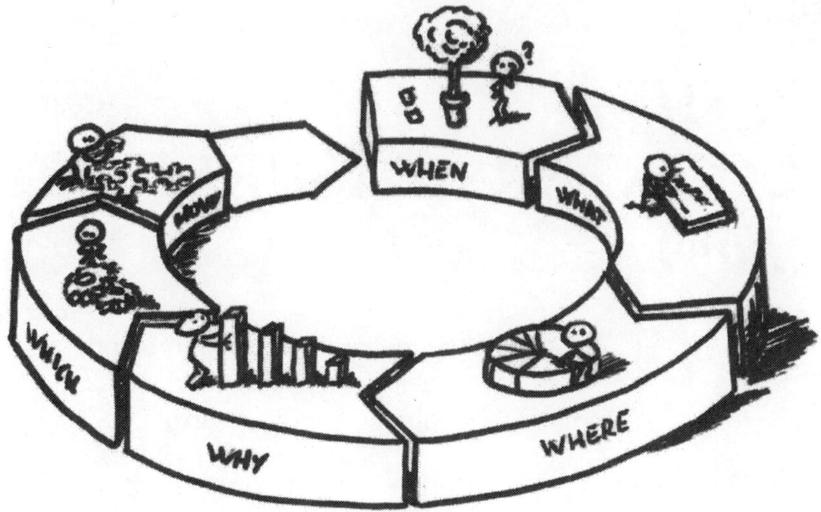

Fig:7.1: The APS doughnut: How

The Countermeasures

Now that we have identified what the root causes are, we have also isolated the MIN processes that need to be fixed; it's now time to proceed with the identification of countermeasures, those actions required to ensure that each of the root causes cease to exist.
Later we will discuss about the effectiveness of countermeasures. Now it is sufficient to keep in mind that the possibility a problem has to reappear is always present. For this reason, the countermeasures must be applied continuously and effectively to ensure that the problem does not reappear anymore.

Moreover, if we accept the postulate that there are many problems and for each of them there are several countermeasures running simultaneously, it is quite obvious to assume that the world around us is full of active countermeasures against potential problems.

Normally there are many more countermeasures than our eyes are able to discover at first sight.

Permanent Countermeasures

Let's begin to explore the concept of a countermeasure. Etymologically, countermeasure means "measure - against", a voluntary action against the perpetration of the cause in time.
Defined this way the countermeasure has the following characters:

- Voluntariness
- Duration
- Effectiveness (in acting against the cause)

The countermeasure is therefore an action on the existing system or process that lasts permanently.
For this reason, these countermeasures are normally defined permanent countermeasures.

Temporary Countermeasures

Most of the problem solving methodologies, however, use to define "countermeasures" both the permanent and the temporary activities, That is arguable because the temporary are only intended to quickly bring the situation within acceptable limits but in the meantime lack the character of "permanence" and therefore cannot ensure the problem won't reappear in future.
These temporary countermeasures are missing two out of the three characters of a well-made countermeasure: they are not durable and do not solve the Root Cause, they just make the problem bearable for what can be done with a quick action.

Although an argument purely related to terminology, this is a point where typically a lot of misunderstandings happen between the people working on solving problems.
The whole thing is powered by a misuse of terms, which unfortunately is widespread among the major problem solving methods when describing the temporary countermeasures. This terminology enables the error, making it difficult to understand. Confusing the temporary action with a real, permanent countermeasure also means opening the door to failure, to

realising, sometimes too late, that the Root Cause has not been properly managed.

Let's take a strong and easy example to understand this concept better.

If I suddenly cut my arm off with a band saw, one of those that are used to cut pieces of wood in the sawmills, the first thing I have to do is stop the bleeding and get immediately treated to prevent death by exsanguinations.
Stanch the bleeding is a temporary action, so by definition it is not a countermeasure because it lacks the characteristic of being durable in preventing the problem reoccurring the future. Moreover, it is also not a countermeasure as it lacks in being effective against the Root Cause. When I'm stopping the bleeding I'm not preventing my other arm from being cut off in the future.

This example may seem trivial but it is certain that, if we do not understand the difference between countermeasures and normalisations, it will be difficult to carry out problem-solving activities with success.

Going back to the example we just analyzed, after having the normalisation applied and being able to quickly get back to the acceptable conditions (i.e. life is not in danger anymore because the risk of continuous bleeding has been managed), it is necessary to identify which are the real countermeasures, the permanent ones.
Those countermeasures, thanks to their effectiveness, their duration and their voluntariness, are necessary to eliminate or to prevent the root causes from recurring again in the future. The result is that the same problem doesn't reappear again.

We must therefore study how to eliminate the possibility that those who work or come close to the band saw in our example might inadvertently or carelessly cut themselves again, very seriously. This possibility cannot be absolutely guaranteed by the temporary countermeasure to stop the bleeding, but must be removed by one or more permanent countermeasures (true countermeasures) that voluntarily, permanently and effectively ensure the elimination of the root causes.

The differentiation of the countermeasures in "temporary" and "permanent" has served us to understand how they are commonly defined and understand how they are treated by other problem solving methods.

Normalisations

In my opinion we need to stop talking about "countermeasures" in the case of temporary solutions, to avoid the risk of getting confused. To reinforce the model in which true countermeasures are only the permanent ones, I strongly believe that the best approach is to call the other actions as "normalisation" to avoid the creation of a false illusion that they may represent countermeasures against the recurrence of the problem.

Defining "Normalisations" those temporary actions can help to identify permanent and effective countermeasures, without expecting miracles from other actions that do not act "against" the root causes.

After having the meaning and usefulness of countermeasures and normalisation defined, it is good to deal with how to identify the actions to be performed.

A phase of the search for solutions to be applied, whether they are normalisations or countermeasures, may benefit from a brainstorming session or similar techniques to search for ideas and build consensus. Brainstorming is a kind of meeting in which a group of people look for solutions without suffering negative influences that may derive from the comments of other participants or negative climate in the team.
In this type of meeting it is forbidden to judge the other ideas, but try to enable everyone to contribute to a spontaneous "flow

of ideas". Also crazy ideas are welcome.

Among the most effective and popular methods to perform a brainstorming session there are the CSM and the classic brainstorming approaches.

CSM: Crawford Slip Method

This method was invented by dr. D.C. Crawford of the University of Southern California in the '20s and is still used and mentioned in several publications.
This method is a fast and economic technique that aims towards the production of individual brainstormed ideas. Individuals do not come in contact with each other during the creation of ideas and this aspect facilitates anonymity and the free flow of proposals without filters that may arise by the fear of being judged.

The ideas are created in the following way: the group must be led by a facilitator. The facilitator will indicate to the team that they need to respond to 10 questions he will raise in sequence every minute. The answers must be written by all members of the team on sticky notes of the same color, which were previously assigned to everyone, without talking to each other.

The speed of the method and the ban of speaking prevents potential discussions from birth and force the members of the team to focus on the research for ideas.
After being asked the first question, each team member will write the answer on the sticky note #1, the same happens with the second question on the sticky note #2, going on with the third, fourth, etc., until all the answers have been written down and collected.

The facilitator starts to ask the first question "how can we eliminate the identified root cause?" He then wait for a minute so that each member of the group can write their own idea, in silence, on the first sticky note. Then he continues with question

number 2: “how can the identified root cause be eliminated?”, and waits again even if the question is redundant. The facilitator keeps on repeating the same, or a similar, question every minute forcing people to look for new ideas to work on.
At the end of the 10 minutes he will probably have obtained dozens of ideas. Each sticky note will be fixed to a blackboard, in bulk, in order to ensure anonymity and the categorisation of ideas can take place, shifting similar ideas in similar positions on the board, so groups of similar ideas can be obtained, thus creating an affinity diagram.

A subsequent discussion of what is in the affinity diagram helps to identify small groups on which to make further assumptions or additional risks that may come to mind when reading the ideas of others.

Classic Brainstorming

There are two versions: "in loop" and "in parallel". In both you have people around a table, with sticky notes and pens to write. Having shown a single root cause, you ask the group to write the solutions, taking care to divide them into normalisation and countermeasures, without thinking to hierarchical and cultural differences between members of the same team. Usually a fairly short time limit is given in order to stimulate a quick flowing of ideas to entice members of the team not to censor themselves for any reason.

In the "in parallel" approach each team member writes down ideas on the sticky notes during the limited time at his disposal, while in the "in loop" approach every member has the opportunity to put on the table, one note at a time, at the moment it is asked in rotation among all team members.

The "in loop" approach is the one that deviates more from the CSM method as it stimulates the birth of new ideas from those that have already been placed on the table by others, a situation that cannot occur at the moment until the members make all their ideas visible at the same time.

The sense of brainstorming activities can be better understood from this story that, even though I'm not able to verify if it has really happened, it allows us to grasp the message in a very effective way.

In a clothing trading company were occurring thefts of goods during off hours. Although the company was equipped with anti theft systems and alarm connected to the police, all the thefts were completed within a few minutes so that the police had never been able to intervene in time to catch the thieves and thwart theft.

At a late-evening meeting, in which the directors of the company were looking for a solution, a member of the cleaning staff had obtained the permission to proceed with the restoration of the meeting room even though it was still occupied by the meeting, and was then involuntarily listening to the description of what happened.

Spurred by the belief that he could have a solution to propose, the cleaner asked and actually obtained the opportunity to speak up about his solution which consisted of alternating hook directions by which the clothes hangers are stored, so that they were alternately suspended and it should have been made difficult to remove the hangers by grabbing all the clothes in bulk, an action that probably allowed the thieves to be fast and effective that far.

The plan was positively evaluated and adopted so that in the following theft the thieves lost precious minutes in removing all the clothing in bulk. They were finally captured and the cleaner attendant was awarded a prize for the simple but brilliant idea.

The Opportunity Matrix

Once we have gathered the ideas, whether they are linked with CSM or brainstorming, but especially after they have been divided between normalisation and countermeasures, we can proceed to their categorisation through the use of the "opportunity matrix" to look for the appropriate actions to be performed.

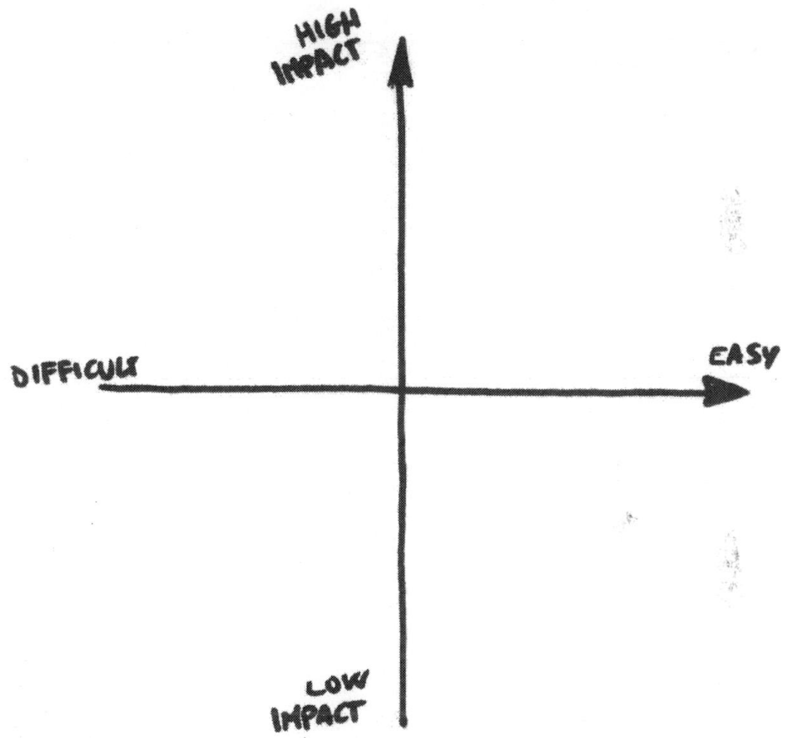

Fig: 7.2: The structure of the opportunity matrix

The matrix is the final step that satisfies the research for the "how". How can any root cause be eliminated?

For each root cause we should carry out a CSM or brainstorming session and in each session we collect and place the sticky notes on the matrix in the most relevant quadrant.

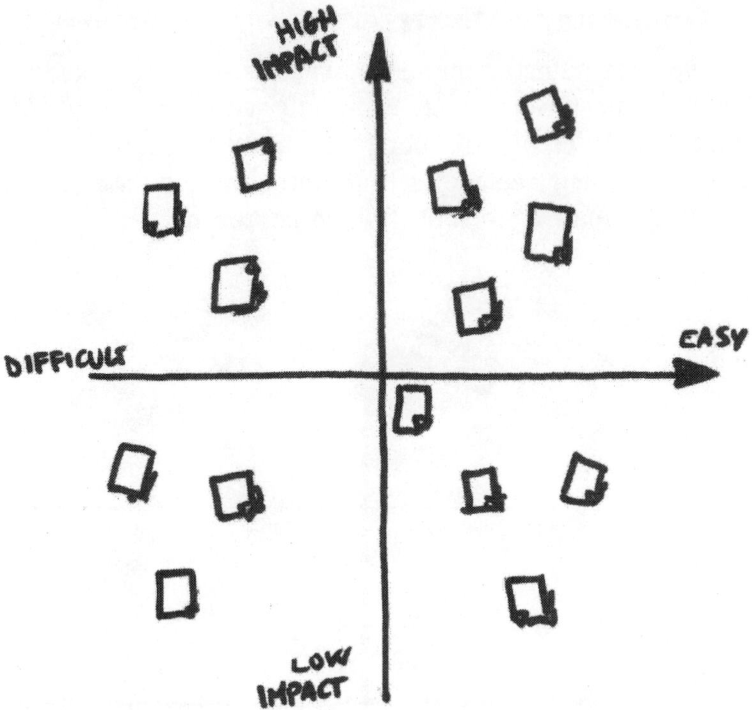

Fig: 7.3: The Opportunity Matrix

The array of opportunities is made up on the left-right direction of the horizontal axis (the x-axis) with the increasing ease of application of the proposed solution, and bottom up on the vertical axis (the y-axis) with the estimated impact that each idea has in contributing to fix the gap (sometimes solutions may cover more than onc root cause, that's why is good to refer to the problem's gap).

Do, Plan, Evaluate, Forget

The top right quadrant, the one that contains the easy to apply ideas which have an expected high impact is also known in jargon as the "magic quadrant".

In it we find all the ideas that must be applied quickly without discussing too much about, it is the area of initiatives to DO!

The top left quadrant contains ideas that are less easy to apply but since have high-impact require careful planning; it is the area of initiatives to PLAN.

The lower right quadrant contains the ideas easy to be implemented but with an expected low impact, ideas that we can possibly reconsider at a later time if the ideas of the previous two areas are proven to be insufficient to close the gap; it is the area of ideas to EVALUATE.

The last one in the lower left quadrant contains ideas difficult to apply with a little or no impact, that's the area of initiatives to FORGET about.

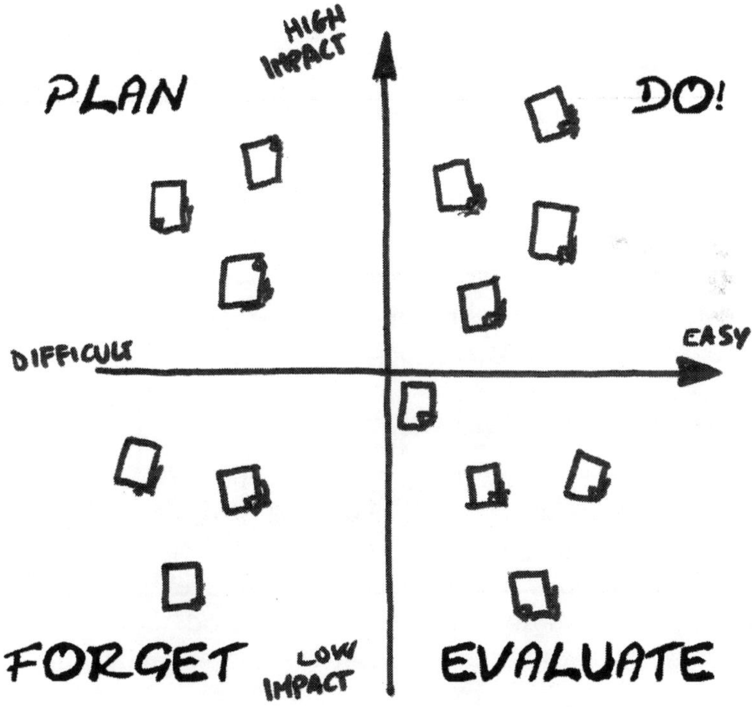

Fig: 7.4: The Matrix and the action types

Normally, the ideas collected through any brainstorming or CSM session provide in a short time many indications of what is important to do to fix the problem.

What is very rare is to find the people who are able to "make things happen". This is a matter of a clear understanding of the following point: these ideas, albeit collected by a method, satisfy the concept of what have to be done, but do not meet the "how to do it".

To fill this gap and to reorganise ideas by collecting also the suggestion on "how to do it", it is necessary to learn by looking further into what the theory says about the effectiveness of countermeasures, with implicit reference to the category of permanent countermeasures, the real ones.

We are not considering here the normalisations which can be "quick and dirty" and by far they do not have to be carefully selected since we do not have to take care of their sustainability.

People often may mistakenly believe they have completed their work just by identifying what should be done; in such cases, without concrete actions, the solution remains useful only *in theory*, while the problem continues to survive *in practice*.

To Make Things Happen

There are not so many problem solving methods which satisfy exhaustively the chapter of countermeasures effectiveness and their sustainability. Especially the high level managerial or university methods tend to cater more the feeling of personal satisfaction of those who study the method rather than the effectiveness of the research and application of countermeasures in reality to eliminate the problem at its roots, forever.

The maturity of those who solve real problems is challenged by this approach; what I can assure you is that your self-esteem and personal fulfillment grow much more when solving problems happens in the real world rather than being pampered during an expensive but just theoretical approach that aim fixes the world's problems through PowerPoint slides. The fix of real problems will allow you to become *a leader that makes things happen.*

For these reasons, from this point on, the book covers topics that may not be well known to other people who may have already been through problem solving methodologies that, unfortunately, have a weak approach to the effectiveness of countermeasures and how to make things happen.

In the future, by talking about problem solving or resolving real problems with other people who have studied different methods, you may feel or see in them the under-evaluation of the importance of countermeasures.

With that said, in order to make things happen, you'll probably need to raise awareness among your colleagues or teammates about the importance of this part of the method that they may tend to forget or simply don't know.
One thing remains sure, always keep in mind that the problems will never be resolved by presentations projected in a meeting room.

Therefore, by hearing people that say, after having found a solution, they applied it as "they told someone to act", "they wrote an e-mail" or "they have updated the procedure", we will realise immediately to be in front of people who did not understand that to make things happen takes a lot more.

In this "HOW" chapter we have covered how we can identify countermeasures and select those most important to invest time and money on. In the next chapter "HOW MUCH" we will discuss the delicate subject of how effective are the countermeasures in order to raise awareness about the effectiveness, which depends a lot on how they are implemented.

8. EFFECTIVENESS OF COUNTERMEASURES *(how much)*

Goal	Understanding the characteristics that countermeasures must have in order to be truly effective. Identify which type of countermeasure requires monitoring and which are self-sustaining.
Content 	• The Effectiveness of Countermeasures • The Scale of the Effectiveness • How to Build a Countermeasure • Countermeasures at the Gas Station • Poka Yoke Countermeasures • Prevention and Detection

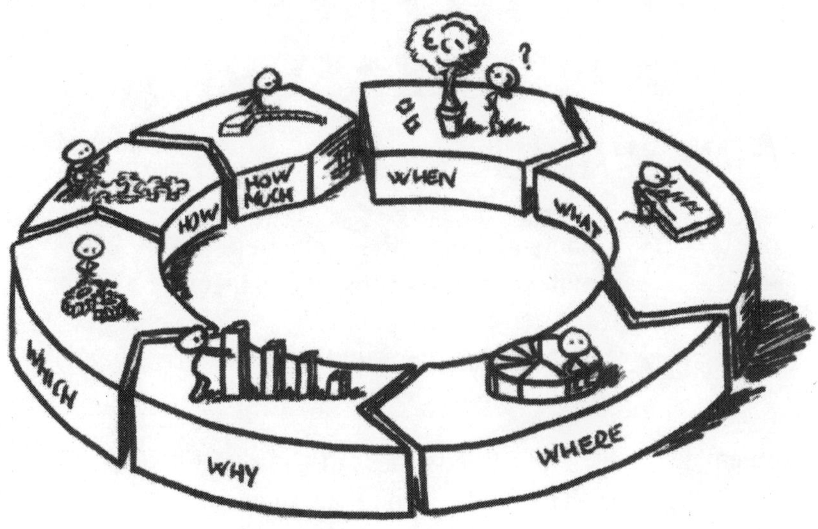

Fig: 8.1: The APS Doughnut: How Much

The Effectiveness of Countermeasures

The study of the effectiveness of countermeasures is crucial for being successful problem solvers. This is precisely the point at which the problem solving methodologies fall down. This part of the Applied Problem Solving method aims to fill some of the gaps which, as already noted, are unfortunately part of purely theoretical approaches.

The value added of carrying out the problem solving lies in identifying the most effective and self-sustaining countermeasures, as it is through them that the root causes will be managed and prevented. Otherwise they will recur and start to feed the problem tree again.

To be poorly effective at this stage, which comes at the end of the analysis, is a waste of opportunities at first, and a waste of money and time at second if we think of the work we've done so far.

Let us get back to our method. How should we look for countermeasures to develop our ability in identifying the most effective ones?

Let's not forget that the countermeasures are only those that act at the root causes level; these are the only actions that are useful to undertake and to ensure that the problem won't reappear in the future. We are not speaking about normalisations in this part of the method.

The Scale of Effectiveness

First of all it is good to distinguish between countermeasures by the amount of probability they offer in fixing the root cause of the problem, aiming to eliminate it at 100%.

Different methodologies have attempted to explain this aspect, a quite common metric came out, expressing through a scale the increased effectiveness from type to type:

- No countermeasure
- simple communication
- procedure / written method
- training
- visible warning sign
- process that includes the countermeasure
- process that cannot be completed without complying with the countermeasure
- error proof process (distraction proof process)

Entering into every nuance does not move the needle that much; what matters is to understand how to be effective in implementing a successful countermeasure. The goal, sometimes ambitious, must be to always look for a countermeasure that is as much as possible at the end of the list which we have just seen.

Also this time the APS approach tends to deviate slightly from traditional approaches, towards a more simple and effective methodology to the problem solver's job.
We are in a phase that is, by its nature, a very specific phase, a phase in which different problems, at this point, are leading us to very different solutions.

Although with the support of the methods, being able to move on with this very specific phase becomes more and more difficult. For this reason, the suggestion is to reconsider all the points in the list and group them into three broad categories so we do not disperse our attention by chasing too many details.

Let's consider this list, deliberately reduced:

- Countermeasures related to the knowledge of the user
- Countermeasures related to the will of the user
- Countermeasures related to the process

The combination of the latter two is more powerful, much more powerful than the last one alone, let's see why.
The latest countermeasure related to the process is the most effective, especially when it is a countermeasure built into the process in order to deliberately create a situation in which it is impossible to continue in case of error or distraction. Countermeasures of this type are very effective, and to identify the best one we must also take into account the will of the user.

How to Build Up a Countermeasure

Knowing the wishes of the user will always make it easier to identify which is the point in the process where the countermeasure will be truly effective.
The approach that APS proposes is the following.
We must:

- identify what the user wants to do
- identify possible errors at each stage
- handle errors before fulfilling the need of the user.

Here are some simple examples related to everyday life.

We need to apply a countermeasure to prevent the user from forgetting the credit card when going to the ATM to withdraw cash.
The best countermeasure is: do not allow to meet the needs of the user if he is making mistakes.

Requirement: withdraw cash.
Potential error: to forget the credit/debit card.
Solution: force the user to take back the card from the machine before providing the cash.

This solution has been applied widely and has dramatically reduced the percentage of forgotten cards. This solution has not ruled out entirely the possibility to forget the card, there are also a few cases in which the user forgets the cash as well, but this is an unmanageable case as the user may have changed its own wishes during the execution of process. Thanks to this the percentage of users who forget the card has been reduced back to acceptable limits so the problem can be considered solved. Are we saying that with this solution the money may be lost along with the card if the user doesn't take the card back?
No, also this exception is handled, once more applying the described method.
The scenario has changed, let's check it out:

Requirement: Do not lose money and card.
Potential failure: the user forgets to take the cash, or for any reason cannot continue the operation.
Solution: warn the user that if the money is not taken away from the ATM within a reasonable time limit (some seconds) the transaction will be canceled by activating the automatic withdrawal of cash.

In similar scenarios, there are also weaker countermeasures in place, such as those that warn the user with messages during the execution of the activity. These countermeasures, however, are

ideally implemented to manage less serious events, like an error in pressing buttons so the process is canceled and must be repeated.
Let's see other cases.

Countermeasures at the Gas Station

A similar case can be analyzed at the gas station.

Requirement: supply the car with fuel, a flammable and explosive liquid, in a safe way.
Potential error: to forget the credit card during the self service prepayment authorisation.
Solution: Return the card to the user without enabling the fuel supply until the card is not voluntarily removed from the slot (similar to ATM).

Then, there may be other errors?
Let's see ... another error would be the fuel type or the number of the pump, an error that can be intercepted before allowing the fuel load.

Requirement: You want to refuel the car by using the pump close to your vehicle.
Potential error: realising that you have not selected the right pump or the right type of fuel.
Solution: automatic cancellation of the transaction, if the refuel is not made within a given time.

Also what about if the user does not notice the error and tries to refuel the vehicle anyway?

Requirement: The user wants to refuel
Potential error: wrong pump or wrong fuel type
Solution: If the pump is not the correct one the fuel cannot be spilled out from the pump; if the fuel is of the wrong type (Petrol vs. Diesel) the nozzle of the pump cannot be entered into the fill spout.

This is an example in which the standardisation of size and shape of the fill spouts of the vehicles and the pump nozzles allows us to manage a certain type of error, as to refill the vehicle with the wrong fuel.

Diesel fuel cannot be plugged into an unleaded petrol vehicle because the nozzle is bigger than the fill spout. It is possible to do the opposite, anyway this is the less dangerous case; we can put unleaded petrol in the Diesel car without damaging the engine, while the diesel fuel into a petrol car damages the engine. Moreover, there are situations in which you may want to fill the vehicle with a fraction of petrol in a diesel vehicle to prevent the fuel from freezing when the external temperatures are far below the freezing point.

If it had been the other way round as well as dangerous, would refueling a diesel car with unleaded petrol have been easy to be managed with a different solution which prevents the error in both cases?

Should you be asked tomorrow for a different solution to manage both errors, unleaded petrol into a diesel car and vice versa, can you indicate a more restrictive resolution than the one currently implemented?

Could it be the shape of the nozzle, sized appropriately? A square cross-section would not fit in a rounded fill spout, and a round section nozzle would not fit in a squared fill spout. Some kid's games are based on this concept to develop child's ability to understand the go-no go concept.

Error handling does not stop here: what happens if the user grabs the fuel pump by immediately squeezing before reaching the fill spout?

Requirement: allow to dispense the fuel without losing liquid, in a fire safe way.

Potential failure: the user inadvertently squeezes the pump before entering the nozzle into the fill spout, causing himself to get wet with fuel, a very annoying and dangerous situation.

Solution: dispense the fuel only after a few seconds of delay to prevent the leakage of liquid that may occur before reaching the opening.

And then, which other mistakes can we intercept?
Definitely the next one may be not to notice that the tank is full and continue to dispense fuel over the tank capacity, outside the vehicle.

Requirement: delivering fuel to the maximum tank capacity but no more.
Potential error: the excess may spill out of the vehicle in an attempt to fill up over the maximum capacity, wasting fuel and creating a fire hazard.
Solution: a mechanism to automatically shut down the flux of fuel at the time the fuel is likely to leak out because the tank is full.

Another possible mistake is to leave behind the fuel cap somewhere at the gas station.

Requirement: do not forget the fuel cap after having filled the vehicle.
Potential error: put the cap on the vehicle roof or on another surface at the gas station and then forget it once the fuel requirement has been satisfied.
Solution: Avoid the cap can be physically separated from the vehicle, by linking it with a rope or chain to the vehicle, or by creating a system to cover the fill spout without the use of a cap.

It's not over here, in the worst case the user fills up and may forget to remove the nozzle from the fill spout before moving the vehicle away; what would happen in this situation?

Requirement: leave the pump safely.
Potential error: forgetting the nozzle is still in the fill spout and move the vehicle away.
Solution: install a hose with a predefined failure point, a point

in which the hose has the weakest resistance to traction and a safety valve which stops the flow in case of breakage of the hose (exactly the case in which the vehicle leaves and rips the pump off from the gas station).
Thanks to this countermeasures have become possible to give everybody a chance to safely refuel vehicles, with an acceptable residual risk for their health and for the health of other customers, without physical assistance, without having to study a manual, without needs of any attitudinal tests, furthermore without any formal training.

Handling flammable liquids in a high risk area like the gas station has become in our life a very safe activity.

An effective countermeasure satisfies the requirement only after the successful management of each possible errors

That's a big win in the method over the human fallacy. It's actually as easy as buttering a slice of bread at breakfast time. In the absence of the analysis of user requirements it should have been difficult to catch and handle all possible errors. The more we keep the sequence of the activities under control, the easier it will be to identify possible errors and to manage them through an "error-proof" approach. Error proof countermeasures are also known with the Japanese term "Poka-Yoke"[15], which means error-proof countermeasures.

[15] The definition of error-proof, in Japanese, was originally developed as Baka-Yoke, literally "fool-proof", a definition that has been changed because was politically incorrect. Beyond the redefinition of the term that might seem offensive in its original version, it was important to change the definition to restore the concept that is not by blaming someone (the fool) that the problem is solved, but considering how the process can be changed so that anyone, perhaps casually, can make mistakes without effects on the problem.

Poka-Yoke Countermeasures

A good way to tell if you have taken distraction-proof countermeasures, or Poka-Yoke, is to apply intelligence to the process and try to answer the simple question: "Can I take a picture of the intelligence of the process?"

Shigeo Shingo[16] introduced the Poka-Yoke concept in 1961 during his career at Toyota.
Poka-Yoke mechanisms serve to secure an entire process. The presence of Poka-Yoke solutions ensures that the correct conditions are always monitored and guaranteed so as to avoid the appearance of defects in the broad sense.

Whether it is not possible to fulfill the elements of a Poka-Yoke prevention function, we need to think of a function that detects problems before they become serious and painful (a concept that moves towards a more Japanese approach called Jidoka[17]).

Despite our carefulness we must always be directed toward finding error-proof solutions, in addition to Jidoka solutions.
Further actions that help to manage the root cause can be identified from the following categories:

- Redundant control systems (more controls operating in parallel, according to different principles, can report in a different way about the detection of mistakes)
- Maintenance programs (where countermeasures can be bypassed or circumvented by the user, like removing safety protection or non-wearing personal protection

---

[16] Japanese engineer known for introducing the Poka-Yoke concept and the SMED method to get faster production change over on the production lines in order to make the work less expensive for small batches compared to mass production.

[17] Jidoka means automation with a human touch, otherwise known as autonomation. It is a technique of automatic stop of processes as soon as the standards are not met anymore. The human can then intervene to restore the proper functioning of the process and no defects are delivered as output.

equipment, maintenance schedules or audits may identify and suggest the need to restore the situation as should be)

- Mitigating risks (probability studies of individual risks, such as FMEA[18], resulting in mitigation of the worst ones, may be important where it is not possible to apply a completely error proof solution)

It is not true, as many individuals may think, that the Poka-Yoke aids are only electrical or electronic devices performing automatic checks during the execution of the process. Often the most effective solutions are mechanical or visual, so they are measures that constrain the freedom of being able to do something in other ways than the correct one, or that make very visible the misuse or the mistake itself.

Prevention and Detection

Should we need to divide the most effective systems of applying the countermeasures into categories, we could think of two groups: prevention systems and detection systems.

Prevention systems are methods and/or workflows that ensure it will be impossible to continue with the process in case of anomalies. Alternatively, if this is not feasible, we can adopt methods that force the user to clearly notice the anomaly, leaving to the individual the ultimate decision of deciding what to do.

Needless to say, the first method is more effective.
The detection systems are usually involved in cases where it is not possible to implement prevention systems.

These systems are monitoring systems that ensure the correctness of execution, alerting in case of anomalies.

---

[18] Failure Mode and Effect Analysis, is the study of the possible problems that may happen, linking the likelihood together with the severity of the consequences, in order to identify those that deserve action to bring them within acceptable limits.

Examples would be the anti-theft systems in stores, rulers, calipers and colors that help us to understand whether the operation was carried out in the correct way, and many other systems as we shall see in Chapter 11, in which we will examine some existing Poka-Yoke systems.

9. SUSTAINABILITY OF RESULTS *(sustain)*

Goal

How to maximise the benefits of countermeasures that last over time, knowing and identifying the need and the way to monitor their effectiveness.

Content

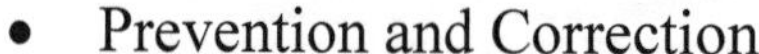

- Prevention and Correction

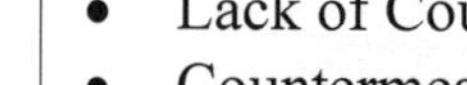

- Lack of Countermeasures

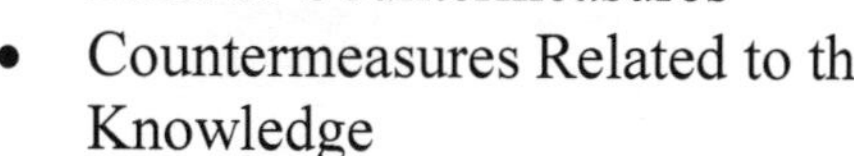

- Countermeasures Related to the Knowledge
- Countermeasures Related to the Will
- The Balance of Power Between the Parties
- Countermeasures Related to the Process

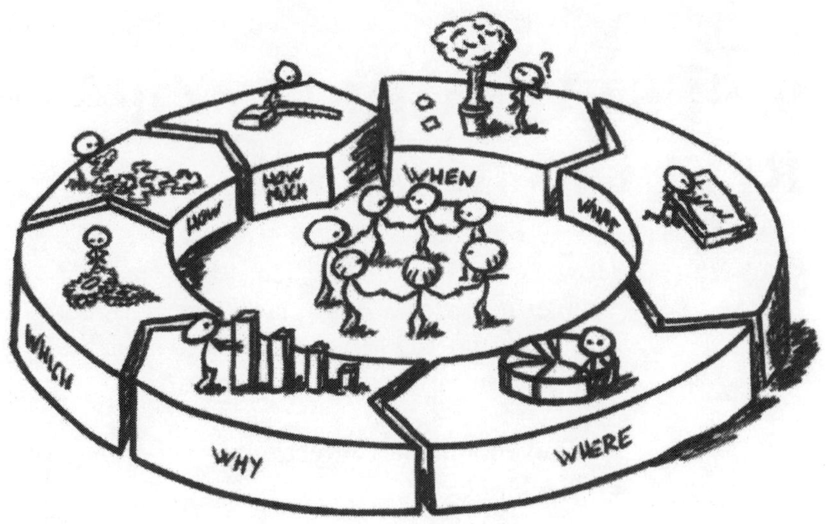

Fig: 9.1: The completion of the APS Doughnut: Sustain the results

Prevention and Correction

Looking for sustainable countermeasures is very important to avoid the problem from reoccurring in the future.

We have seen that Poka-Yoke countermeasures are effective because they force us to handle the error before it happens. Other countermeasures, albeit less effective, warn on failure to allow for immediate resolution.

If the Poka-Yoke countermeasure is of solid construction, so it is not easily circumvented by those who might commit the error, then we will not have to worry about ensuring the sustainability of the solution.

In other words, the solution is self-sustainable.

The example that we made earlier about possible errors in refueling the vehicle contains many examples of Poka-Yoke solutions that are self-sustaining:

- The automatic stop of the fuel dispensed when the tank is

full is inescapable and cannot be disabled by the user with other techniques.

- Returning the card before delivering the fuel is automatic and inescapable .
- The supply of diesel in the car running unleaded petrol is by-passable by the user, however, requires the use of a funnel or an additional connector, which is an activity that can go wrong only if you do want to make the mistake and you organise yourself to make it voluntarily.
- Forgetting the tank cap is no longer possible and, at worst, we will drive with the tank open, but the cap will not get lost.
- Dispense fuel earlier while trying to insert the fuel dispenser into the tank, is a mistake that is prevented by the delay in the delivery of the fuel.

The other errors are not yet the subject of prevention but correction:

- Selecting a dispenser far away from our car will be fixed by the system because there will be no refueling for a given period of time. The error is not prevented but it won't end up with an economical loss for the user.
- Starting without removing the dispenser from the tank opening is not prevented but is corrected by the safety valve which prevents the gas station from being flooded by flammable liquids.

Note that at this stage we are not separating cases in which the error is due to distraction from those in which the error was committed voluntarily. There is an advantage to consider them together. By grouping them together we leverage our ability to find solutions effective most likely in both cases.

Any other solution that is not self-sustaining needs further follow-up activities to monitor their contribution and to intervene if the countermeasure is not effective and does not last in time.

If countermeasures are not self-sustaining they will have to be measured one by one

I urge you to always and incessantly look for all the possible Poka-Yoke approaches for your countermeasures.

The reason is simple: most of the failures in the elimination of problems pass through poorly effective countermeasures, which are, in addition, not lasting in time.

We wrote that the countermeasures can be grouped into the following categories:

- countermeasures related to the knowledge of the user
- countermeasures related to the will of the user
- countermeasures related to the process with increasing levels of efficiency.

Should we need to add something in the first place, then I would say: lack of countermeasures.

Lack of Countermeasures

Let's start from a fundamental point.
To have no countermeasure for every occasion means that we are not always facing a measurable problem, or that we have no rationale to work on countermeasures to solve the issue.

There are several cases in which the absence of countermeasures is the rule rather than the exception. If the problem is absent or not measurable there is no problem and we don't need a countermeasure.

If the gap exists, it is measurable, and we have rationale for it, knowing we do not have an effective countermeasure for the problem should push us towards the identification of an effective action.

If the lack of countermeasures depends on one of the following scenarios:

- Not having enough time
- Waiting for someone else to decide
- Saying "not my job"
- Waiting for "the authority"
- Living with the problem
- Having rationale but waiting, "so it will pass over"

This means we are part of the problem rather than being part of the solutions.

Please do not forget a key point of problem solving: sometimes, in dealing with the problems, we are also allowed to do nothing, provided we do not have rationale, at that time, to solve the problem.

It is important that the absence of a countermeasure is the result of our decision, it must not be an unwanted scenario that suddenly happened.

Countermeasures Related to the Knowledge

When we think about countermeasures, we have to fully understand why those that rely only on the knowledge of the user are very weak. Understanding the cause of these failures will help us to be more effective in "making happen" what we expect to happen.

By redefining this concept, we can say that applying these knowledge based countermeasures does not guarantee the resolution of the problem.

Should the knowledge be enough to avoid the mistakes, which would not be part of human nature, how come is so common we do repeatedly make the same mistakes?
We all know how frequent it is to make the same mistakes and

how common it is to conclude by saying: "I knew this would have happened".

As a consequence we can say that the knowledge alone helps in creating fewer mistakes but does not eliminate the possibility that errors will be committed again and again, and that the problem shows up more and more.
Any countermeasure which bases its effectiveness on increasing the knowledge of the individual is an ineffective countermeasure.

This is very straight forward, ok, it's because the quicker we are in realising that the knowledge of the user is not an effective countermeasure, the better we will become in solving problems without having to always face the same ones.

So if you are thinking about countermeasures similar to those in the list that follows, you must know that your action will not work in a satisfactory manner and will not be sustained over time.

Some ineffective countermeasures based on knowledge of the individuals are:

- saying something
- communicating
- providing instructions
- writing a letter
- writing an e-mail
- writing a procedure
- writing a statement
- hanging a sign
- providing training

If we cannot find any other more effective countermeasures, we at least need to know that the ones listed above will require a lot of energy to be sustained, and will not ensure that the problem disappears.

Let's take the example of the no parking sign for vehicles. Whoever drives a vehicle receives initial training which provides the ability to recognise the meaning of the sign and understands that in its presence the vehicle cannot be parked; when the training is successful a driving license is granted and the individual can start driving and parking the vehicle freely.
Is this enough to avoid having vehicles parked in the wrong areas? No, the result just depends on the rationale of those who are committing the error.

When in presence of the above countermeasures, specific monitoring and controlling actions that consume time and energy are required to ensure the sustainability and the partial effectiveness of these countermeasures.

This range of actions can be summarised in this list:

- Planned Audits
- Meeting
- Conference calls
- Unplanned Audits
- Self-control procedures

and other actions which enable you to maintain the control over the applied countermeasure.

Unfortunately, these activities are effective only during the monitoring phase of the situation. They do not guarantee that the knowledge of the users is being used properly to prevent a recurrence of the problem and are not effective if the monitoring cannot be ensured 24x7.

If we go back to our example of the vehicle parked in the forbidden area, the training of the user has not ensured that no errors are made, however, thanks to the control, these errors can be highlighted to identify the cars illegally parked. We are not yet certain, however, that the no parking rule is sustained over time. What are we missing?

Countermeasures Related to the Will

What is still missing is the adoption of a mechanism that significantly changes the rationale of those individuals who commit the error. If I'm going urgently to the hospital for an emergency I may have many other priorities to worry about other than the no parking sign, so I may not take any notice to that signal as I usually would.

If, however, my rationale is different, for example I'm going out to have a dinner with friends and we are well ahead of time, I may not have enough justifications to allow myself to park in a no parking area. In this case I do not have the rationale.
Moreover, what is valid to me may not be valid for others, due to different priorities, different culture, different education, in other words, everybody is living his own life that is different from each other's.

The key in these types of countermeasures lies in the ability to change the user's rationale making it clear and simple that the mistake will probably generate more problems than it will solve.
To be effective this should work for everyone.

A very simple method is therefore to find a way to channel the hassle to the one who makes the mistake, so he will pay more attention and probably choose an allowed alternative.

> Let's get back again to the example of the no parking sign.
> Thanks to the authority monitoring activities, who makes the mistake will receive a ticket that ends up with an administrative penalty that has an economic impact on his pockets.
> This allows us to change the rationale for some individuals, not for all. Those who are rich enough or for

any reason are not going to pay the fine, they will have their rationale unchanged and will continue to make the mistake.

To improve this solution, there are countries in which the administrative fines are proportional to the declared income of those who get the ticket. In this way, lesser individuals should remain indifferent to the fine, even the richest. However, it remains unchanged the rationale of those who are not going to pay the fine.

Due to this, an approach to change even more the rationale of these people is to generate additional annoyances by clamping the wheels of the car or pulling the car away to generate a logistics pain in addition to the economic one. This may change the rationale also for those individuals that are insensible to the other actions.

Moreover, sometimes to remove the claps takes several hours, and to repossess the car as a result of forced removal is painful because they are released at a deposit poorly served by public transport, located in the suburbs, with the certainty of having to spend money and time to repossess your vehicle.

All of these additional hassles serve to increase the rationale of those who should do things in the right way but unfortunately they do it in the wrong way.

With that said, if we want to solve the problem but have identified only countermeasures related to the knowledge and/or the will of the people, we have to constantly monitor the situation and find ways to transfer the pain to whom is acting mistakenly.

The Balance of Power Between Parties

The following true story makes it possible to understand how to effectively redistribute the annoyance towards the individual that is causing the problem, to fix the situation.

A lady who lives at the first floor of an apartment building has her flat's windows that overlook the garden. Unfortunately it happens that sometimes someone from the upper floor flats throws trash out the window soiling the garden.

The lady, unaware of how to work on sustainable and effective countermeasures, began to face the situation by phone calling the building manager, under the illusion that he can help her through communication to all the people who are living in that building, remembering that everybody is forbidden from throwing trash out the window.

The communication took place without any effect.
Nothing changed, as expected, because the countermeasure was "communication" and we have already seen that is related to the knowledge so it cannot ensure a high effectiveness towards the root cause. If we choose to say or write something hoping that everyone else read the communication, and has rationale to comply with it, we should ask ourselves what happened before, as not throwing things out the window should be part of everyone's civil education.

Not having a real return of the countermeasure, and not having time to wait until the garbage does not accumulate up to reach the individual's window on the upper floors, she had to look for another solution.
The lady then tried to leverage the civic sense of the people by posting a sign on the front door of the building. We can also imagine what the result was: nothing changed, basically it's the same countermeasure to "tell" someone what to do or "write" to someone like in an e-mail giving instructions. To communicate is not

an effective countermeasure.

It was looking for a way to share the pain with the rest of the people in the building that resolved the situation. The lady began to collect a sample of indecent objects every day, putting them in a clear plastic bag and hanging them inside the building in a position where anyone, coming home, would have seen it. Beside the transparent bag a sign explained that a collection of rubbish would have been collected every day until the moment when the launch of rubbish from the upper floors of the building would have ceased.

In two days the story ended up.

One thing is to throw the waste through the window into the garden several feet below our eyesight, another thing is to see every day in front of us the trash when getting back into our apartment. A fully physical growth of the same foul-smelling garbage begins to change the rationale.

In summary, if we cannot find countermeasures better than those related to the individual's knowledge, we need to ensure sustainability through:

1 Issue of the countermeasure
2 Monitoring and measurement
3 Modification of the rationale of those who make the mistake, eventually by sharing the pain.

What we have just seen is part of the logic of the relative strengths - weaknesses of individuals and teams.

A WIN- LOSE situation, where those who make mistakes win and the others lose, it will never be settled as the winner lacks rationale to change his behaviour, and this is just by nature, it is not because they are bad guys.

It is necessary to change the equilibrium in order to create a temporary LOSE - LOSE situation in which even those who commit the error start to suffer the consequences and feel the pain. Only then we can find the consensus needed to emerge stronger from the situation, all motivated to ensure that the error does not happen again, including the faulty individual, by creating a scenario in which both parties win: a WIN -WIN situation.

If we want to restore the balance in power relations between people we must always assess behavioural change. Only communications, even when threatening, are not effective enough.
Let's change our behaviour, let's do it consistently and visibly, and the counterparty will be encouraged to also change its behaviour as reflection.

Should we voluntarily make visible to everybody the result of repeated errors then we will have many possibilities to solve the problem. The bandits are facilitated by the shadow, but in the light of the sun and in front of everyone's eye even the smart ones behave properly.

Countermeasures Related to the Process

During the attempt to identify even more effective countermeasures we normally get closer and closer to the modification of the process that is not working, so we have to look to implement all the measures within the process itself which restricts or inhibits the ability to do things other ways than the correct one.

The strength of these solutions is that they exclude any individual assessment related to the rationale of the people, simply because there are no wrong ways to eventually follow.

Acting right is the price to pay to continue in what we wanted to do or achieve. This class of solutions includes the following:

- Gauges

- Pass / Fail System
- Systems to correct the orientation when couplings objects
- Mandatory fields during data entry
- Systems comparisons
- Dosage for volume
- Automatic weighbridges to interrupt the process
- Photoelectric sensors
- Laser Barriers

Do you find it easier to see how we are approaching the Poka-Yoke concept? If we think about solutions built into the processes, we are taking the correct approach for successful resolutions.

What it takes to be effective is, therefore, a careful analysis of the identified process, an equally accurate identification of risks, and finally the application of measures to ensure that the error is not committed, or that it is immediately reported and fixed.

And then we have to implement the solution. The solutions that are just reports of what's going on or what should be done are not effective at all.

Page intentionally left blank

10. DOCUMENT THE JOB *(A3)*

Goal

Learning how to document our work to maximise the efforts made so far. Collecting the consensus of the other person can solve the problems by relying on everyone.

Content

- The A3 Form
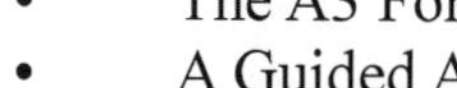
- A Guided A3
- The Header

- The When
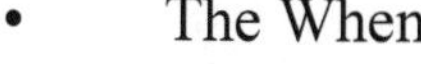
- The What
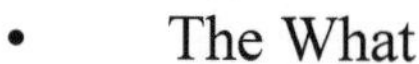
- The Where
- The Why
- The Which
- The How
- The How Much
- Example of A3

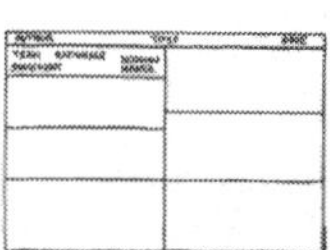

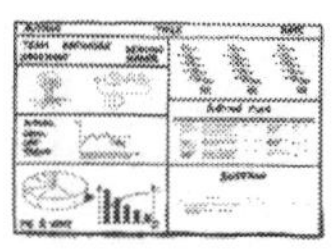

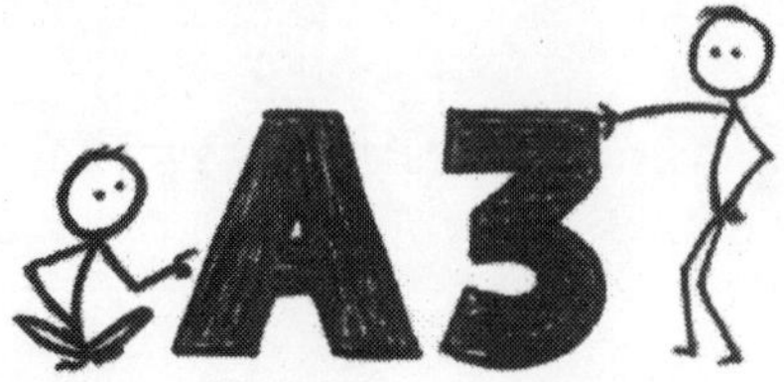

Fig: 10.1: The A3, document the activities to maximise the consensus

The A3 Form

As we have already had the opportunity to comment earlier, the performance of a team working on a problem solving job is very effective when we are able to build a consensus around the activities we are carrying out.

If the problem we are trying to solve is part of the private sphere, it is not essential to document the activities and the analysis that were conducted. For all other cases, however, where the problem to be solved is a problem in the workplace and it is necessary to involve other people, documenting it means we will have much more of a chance of reaching a satisfactory and long lasting solution.

A good job of documenting the carried out investigations and the solutions found is critical to reinforce the consensus that has been created, to leave a written record of what we have decided to do. Having a written report for our boss is useful for future reference so information are transmitted correctly and we avoid that in the future someone will say "but didn't we say that we should have done it differently?".
One of the most popular formats to document the analysis performed during problem solving in the Lean cultures is the A3 form, one of the most common Problem Solving Canvas.

The form takes its name from the A3 paper size, an A3 which measures about 16.5 inches in width and 11.7 in height.

This size or a similar size of paper is readily available in any office and is large enough to accommodate the synthesis of all the outputs of the problem solving activities that have been done.

In Toyota the A3 model has a great diffusion, many books have been written about it. In some organisations has become the way by which the activities should be reported regularly to the upper levels of the hierarchy.

A Guided A3

The content of the A3 form originated in Toyota is relatively "free"; to fill out successfully an A3 requires in this case a good understanding of the problem-solving method and a clear idea of how to properly communicate the analysis and the findings up to the decisions taken.
A free format like this has the advantage of very high flexibility but brings with it the disadvantage of being not so effective in guiding the greenest ones. A free format is otherwise useful to those who are gaining experience. For this reason it is not a real standard, it is the output of a standardised method but this excessive freedom in the use requires a strong experience both by those who wrote it and those who read it.

APS, aiming to simplify things by focusing on the practicality of the method, suggests that we make use of a wizard type version of the A3. This will allow us to be aligned with the A3 standard form, something that will be a benefit for our integration within our organisation (which will increase our effectiveness) and other organisations (which will increase our integration chances through the use of one of the most common standard).

We will see later on step by step how to build the A3 form; This is in line with the contents of A3 that we can find around the globe, but is easier to use because it is guided in its compilation, thanks to a very strict parallelism with the APS method and its phases.

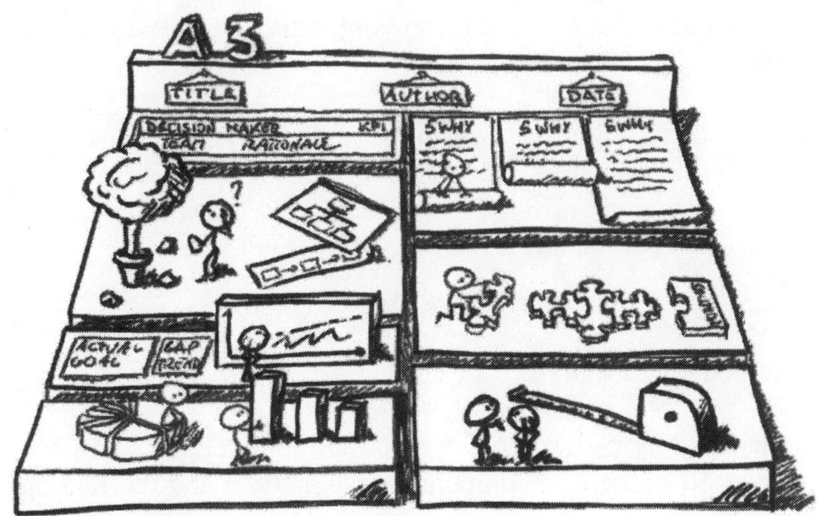

Fig: 10.2: The A3 Template as result of the activities done

The Header

Let's start with the very first step of the APS methodology, the step of defining the problem; we need to ensure that we work on the correct problem. As we have seen, the problem is properly managed in its early stages of definition if we are able to answer the question WHEN, so we are able to put together the puzzle pieces of events according to a time scale that allows us to avoid misinterpretation of the reality.

This phase results in a series of definitions that are documented as:

- Title
- Statement
- Rationale
- Team
- Metrics (actual, goal, gaps, trends)
- Owner
- Decision Maker (if any)

These first pieces of information must be documented using the top area of the A3 template by looking at it landscape, plus the beginning of the first column on the left. Below is an illustration of how it should be divided to adhere to the A3 standard approach.

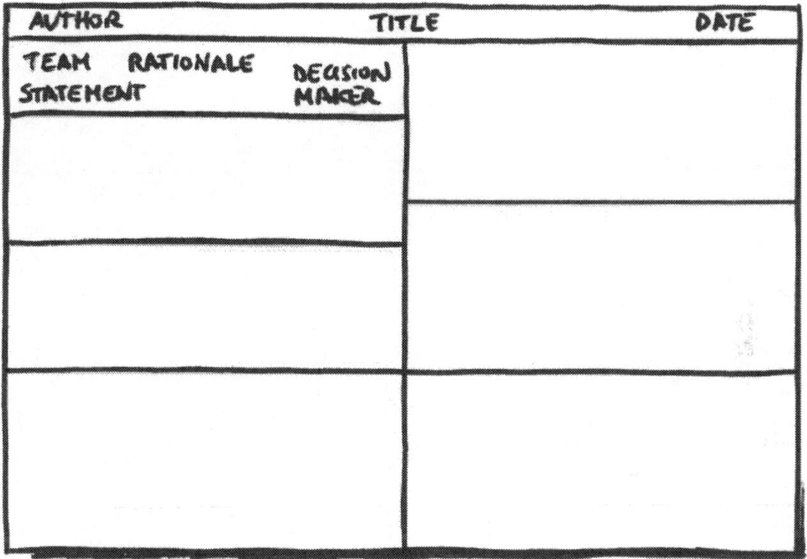

Fig: 10.3: A3, The Background and the Header

This utilisation of the A3 areas adhere to the logic of having a sheet with a title at the top, and two columns on which document from left top-down to right top-down, the activities that have been carried out.

At the top we will put the name of the author (the owner of the A3), the title of the problem (3 or 4 words that allow us to identify the problem later on) and the date when the template was last updated.

Afterwards, going on within the first column, we must write down the name of the problem solving team, insert the statement (two or three lines that describe the problem, including the numbers that define the problem, as the Actual, the Goal, the Gap and the Trend), and finally we will indicate the rationale, a few lines explaining why it is correct that we are the ones that work on this problem.

Example
TITLE: Excessive Waste in Production
AUTHOR: Ivan Fantin
DATE: 15/07/2013

and then

TEAM: Ivan, Julian, Charles, Andrew
STATEMENT: The percentage of rejected parts during the production is too high, we have a goal of 1,000 ppm (parts per million equivalent to 0,1 percent) but we are at 2300 ppm, 1300 ppm is the gap and the trend is stable.
RATIONALE: as Head of Production it is correct that I will take care of this problem, which is worth about $ 130 000 per year as the value of the waste.
DECISION MAKER: Frederick B. (General Manager)

When

To document how we came to understand what happened is the only point in which the use of a guided A3 remains open and flexible.

It may be the need to graphically outline the context of the analysis to make the problem easier to understand. It will then be a matter of using flowcharts, organisation charts, cause-effect diagrams, fishbone diagrams, other charts or any other evidence to support the understandability of the analysis that has been carried out.

The appearance of the A3 starts to become similar to the following example:

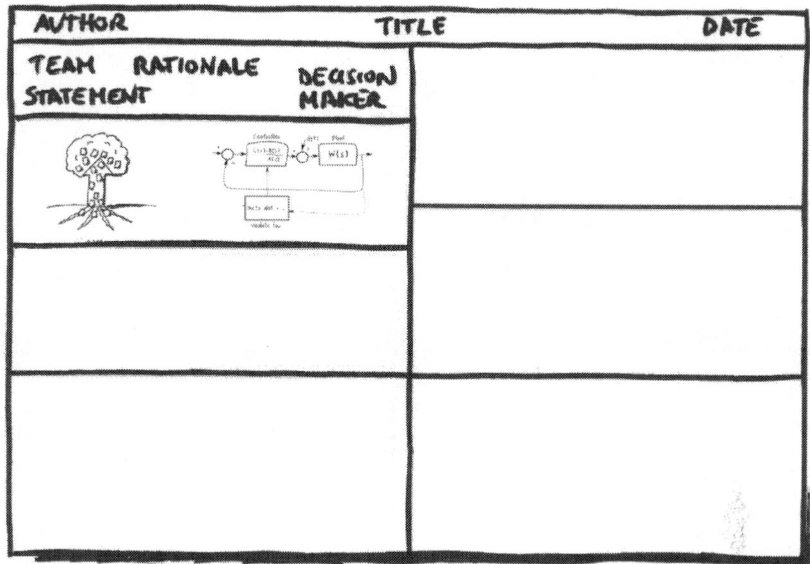

Fig: 10.4: A3, The Background and The Content

After having completed the first part thanks to the WHEN phase, we need to document the answer to the question “WHAT happened?”.

What

Now we enter in the part dedicated to the concerns of "WHAT" happened. This answer is good when represented by the Run Chart as we've already studied, so we dedicate a portion of our A3 to draw the run chart of the problem in which we clearly see if the problem is caused or created, if the gap is very large and if the trend is getting worst, better or is stable. Along with the chart it is also good to write the metrics of problem: Actual, Goal, Gap and Trend.

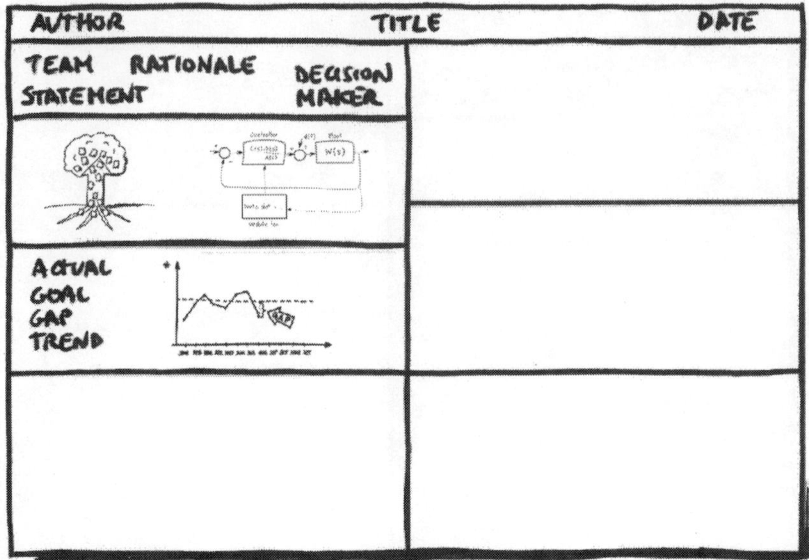

Fig: 10.5: A3, The Background and the Problem Definition

After the Pie Chart, a Pareto histogram represents the contribution of each of the main causes, in other words "WHY" the problem occurred.

Where

After the run chart we can move to the Pie & Why area in which we document the areas of the Pie Chart that represents the number and the importance of each Gemba, “WHERE” is it worth conducting the investigations. On the A3 it appears as in Fig 10.6.

Why

In the same Pie & Why area the Pareto histogram is an excellent way to show the main causes that will be investigated through the Five Whys technique to reach the root cause. At each root cause we will have to find the MIN processes that are responsible for feeding the problem we want to solve.

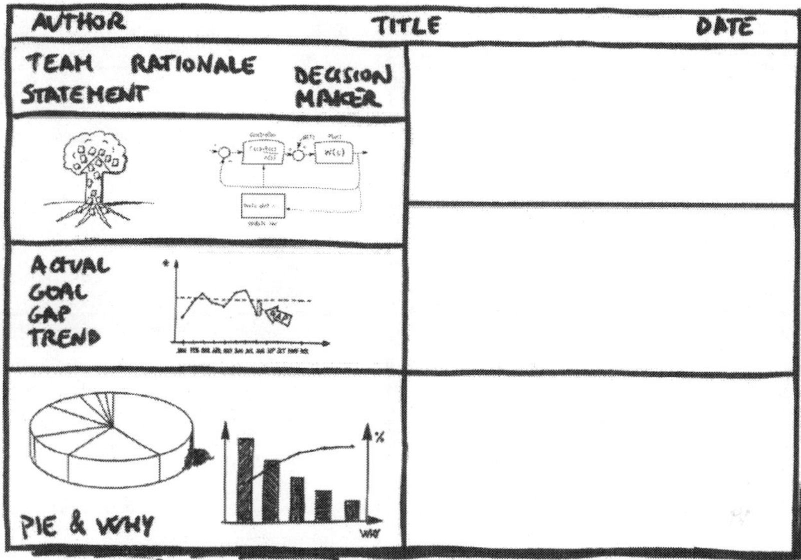

Fig: 10.6: A3, Pie & Why, the Gemba and the Why

Which

The beginning of the second half of the A3 sheet is dedicated to the representation of the Five Why investigation, drilling down to identify "WHICH" are the processes that need to be fixed.

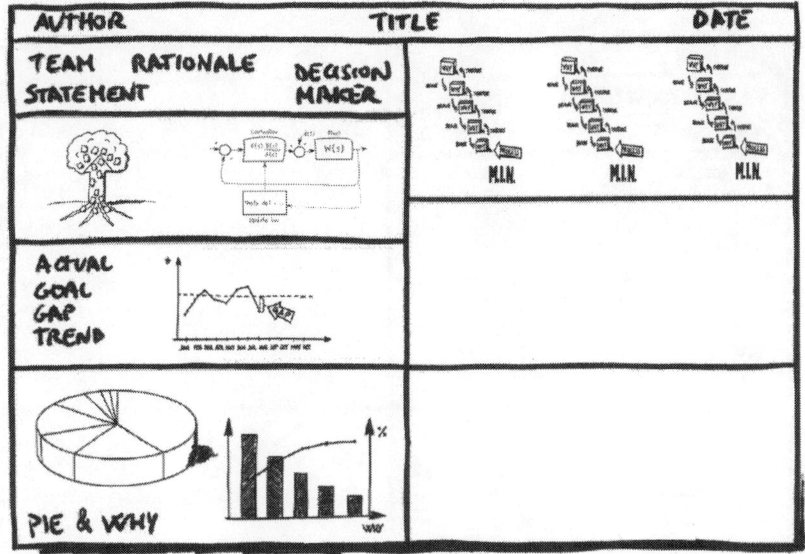

Fig: 10.7: A3, the five whys investigation and the MIN Process

How

We now come to the part where, for each of the identified MIN processes, we can document what are the results of the research of the most effective and easy to implement solutions. This part answers the "HOW" question: how do we eliminate the root causes?

It appears as an action plan in which the elements of the solutions are detailed in a table that contains headers:

- topic
- action
- responsible
- deadline
- status of the update date of the A3

This is the aspect of the A3 that documents the plan of activities requested to solve the problem.

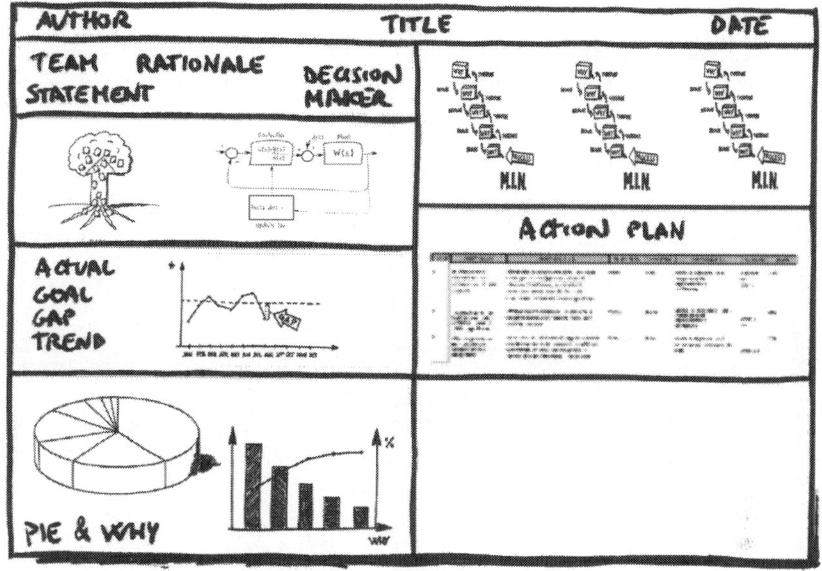

Fig: 10.8: A3, the countermeasures and the action plan

How Much

Now we just have to document how we answer the "HOW MUCH" of the original problem we expect to solve. A new table showing the ways in which we're going to measure the effectiveness of every single individual measure of the action plan will help us in keeping track of all the measurements that we need to put in place for each action that is not implemented as a Poka-Yoke solution (if is a Poka-Yoke is self-sustainable and doesn't need to be monitored).

In this table we report each non Poka-Yoke action in every row, in which we document how we measure the effectiveness of that specific action and what portion of the initial Gap the specific action is supposed to close.

For example, the initial gap was 1300 ppm, we are describing a single action related to the welding station where we can reduce the defect to one half. The result of the implementation of this action is supposed to be the reduction of the original defect rate by half. We must therefore indicate the metric expressing that the partial contribution is 650 ppm.

The table will help also to track the results of the monitoring activity thanks to columns that may measure the results in 30/60/90 days (or whatever time range that make sense for that action and for the problem resolution deadline).

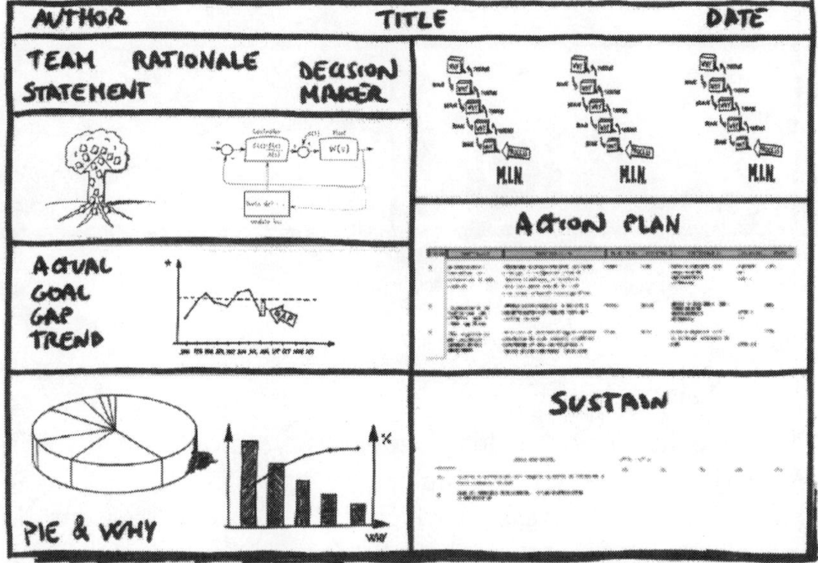

Fig: 10.9: A3, the criteria to measure the sustainability of ach countermeasure

11. EXAMPLES OF SOLUTIONS *(Poka-Yoke)*

Goal	Train our mind and our eyes to identify Poka Yoke inspired solutions in the world in which we live.
Content: Examples	• The Handle • Circular Saws • Household Appliance Blades • Writing Pens • Toner and Cartridges • USB Plugs • Pedestrian Crossings • Public Baths • Cruise Ship Bathrooms • Pay by Card • Hospital Injectable Supplies • American School Buses • Barriers Outside Schools • Computer Messages • The Shoe Method • The Fly • Cold Labels • The Orange Network Cable • The Automatic Transmission • Brake to Start • The Bike Side Stand • Industrial Presses • Laser Barriers • The Parking Maneuver • Seatbelts • An Additional Eye

- Release The Brake!
- Drink or Drive
- Cooking Without Explosions

The opportunity to compare our own ideas with those of other people is a tremendous added value in the moments where we have to find solutions. To have in our team some individuals that have already faced in the past the tricky task of looking for Poka-Yoke solutions, which are distraction proof, is a strong element of value for the whole team.

However, should we not be that lucky, or just as an additional value, we can improve our ability to find solutions also by observing the world around us with different eyes. The new approach should be identifying possible solutions already applied in the past by other people.

Often we do not even realise how many Poka-Yoke countermeasures there are around us; being able to identify these solutions will allow us to understand that, in most cases, it's relatively inexpensive to apply the poka-yoke concept, and this observation of the world will help us to expand our vision.

Example #1: The Handle

Some doors, when installed in public places, are equipped with a "push" or "pull" sign, but that is not enough, people often operate by trials and error as it is instinctively superfluous to read the instructions on how to open a door (who does think of not being able to open a door without receiving directions?).

The Poka-Yoke solution, in this case, can leverage the power of the human instinct: on the side of the door that must be pulled there is a handle that you have to grab, stimulating the instinct to pull it, while on the side of the door that must be pushed the handle is replaced by a flat metal plate, something that can only be pushed as it is not possible to grab it.

The error is not eliminated at 100%, it can be committed only on the side where you have to pull, and then the solution is partially error proof.

An even better solution is represented by the doors of the kitchens in restaurants: the double door is two way, that allows the opening simply by pushing from both sides, eliminating the error to open the door in the wrong direction and it is also hands free for those who may have dishes in their hands.

Requirement: to open the door without guesswork or mistakes.
Potential error: to push or pull, realising that the door opens the other way.
Solution: The shape of the handle drives the behaviour of the user.

Example #2: Circular Saws

A Company called Sawstop produces saws for woodworking. They know very well the danger related to the operations of this type of working equipment in which the operator's hands often handle the wood in a position that is quite close to the cutting point; the big risk is to accidentally touch the blade and cut or amputate parts of the fingers, hands or eventually the arms.

The poka-yoke countermeasure that this company has developed exploits a mechanism of control of the electrical conductivity of what you are cutting: wood is an insulator, the skin conducts electricity as we may experience with the modern touch screens, the blade conducts electricity as it is made of metal.

A sensor detects contact between the blade and a conductor such as a finger or a hand, triggering a mechanism that reacts faster than a car air bag, stopping the blade and preventing cutting the operator.

Requirement: to handle pieces of wood in the same space in which there is an unprotected rotating blade.
Potential error: hitting or touching the blade and then cutting or amputating a part of the arms, hands of fingers
Solution: If the blade is touched by a conductor such as human skin, a mechanism immediately stops the rotation of the blade to avoid injury.

Example #3: Household Appliance Blades

Many appliances and kitchen equipment contain moving blades. The cutting action and breakage in small pieces of food is often carried by blades which would be very dangerous if the body parts come into contact with these parts, especially when in motion.

However, the fact that the blades get dirty requires the users to wash them touching and operating with their hands in their proximity.

It would be an instant to hit inadvertently the on-off switch to create a potential danger, or it might seem convenient for some users to switch on the appliance, cleaning the blade while it is rotating, operating without the original protections in place.

The poka-yoke countermeasure, in these cases, consists in a switch being placed in proximity of the protective parts. This switch is responsible for preventing the appliance from being switched on while the protective parts are disassembled for cleaning activities or other reasons.

Requirement: carrying out cleaning of appliance with protective parts removed.
Potential error: accidentally injury starting the appliance while the protective parts are not in place.
Solution: If protective parts are removed the unit will not start.

Example #4: Writing Pens

Some ballpoint pens, those operated by the “push” button at the end, may have a mechanism that prevents the people, who slip them into the front pocket of their shirt, from getting ink on their shirt because the point is not retracted.

These ballpoint pens have a release mechanism under the tongue that allows the pen to stay in place at the edge of the shirt's pocket. The mechanism causes the return of the ballpoint inside the pen's body in case a piece of tissue is sensed between the tongue and the body of the pen, preventing the ink to drop out or the shirt to get in contact with the ballpoint.

Requirement: putting the ballpoint pen into the shirt pocket.
Potential error: ink on the shirt in an attempt to put a ballpoint pen into the shirt pocket with the tip still exposed.
Solution: If the pen tip has the ballpoint still exposed, the edge of the pocket beneath the clip activates the mechanism of re-entry of the tip.

Example #5: Toners and Cartridges

Have you ever tried to change the toner in laser printers or copiers?

When you open the lid to access the toner, the copier normally goes into stand-by mode, and if during the positioning of the new toner you cannot figure out how to reassemble it correctly, the lid no longer closes, preventing the copier or printer from beginning to work in the presence of evil mounted components.

The danger would be to damage the device, eventually hurting someone or just causing extra time and money to be spent to call the assistance of the manufacturer to handle the problem.

If the user is not blocked while closing the lids, it may be convinced that the printer is ready to print, believing the toner is fitted properly, even if it is unable to print.

Requirement: to properly use the printer without damaging it.
Potential error: the replacement of the toner does not work properly and the printer is damaged or stops working
Solution: If the fixing levers of the toner, and the toner itself, are not positioned correctly the printer cover cannot be closed.

Example #6: USB Plugs

Current computers have I/O ports built according to the standard USB (Universal Serial Bus). These connectors can be used only in one direction. Those who try to insert the connector in the wrong direction will not be able to succeed and will be forced to turn 180 degrees the plug before succeeding. This is one of many examples of driving behaviour through proper forms and the concept of "pass - doesn't pass" criteria, like gauges.

All plugs in the computers are built in this way, starting from the monitor cables, end connector plugs on the network cables, and this works as well with the slots for memory cards and HDMI connections.

Even if the USB is relatively recent, however badly it is designed; we know that you cannot insert the plug into the socket incorrectly, but because its symmetrical shape the users are driven through attempts to proceed because it does not show the correct way of introduction.

Normally, the attempt to insert the USB with the logo facing up allows us to succeed on the first try, but in cases where the socket is mounted vertically and not horizontally the doubt remains and the user is forced to proceed by trial and error.

Requirement: to properly insert a USB plug into the socket
Potential error: to insert it incorrectly and damage the equipment
Solution: make sure that the plug can be inserted only in the correct way

However, what was not handled is the following case:

Requirement: properly insert the USB plug into the socket at the first attempt
Potential error: not understanding what is the correct direction

of insertion and using guess work by trying.
Solution: to visually indicate that both plugs on the outlet have the correct direction of insertion (shapes or colors would work with visual aid)

Solution #2: Apple has managed to create the "Lightning" connector that works when inserted in both possible directions. This is a brilliant solution, unfortunately is not a standard for non-Apple devices.

Additionally, again on the existing USB standard connector, have you ever tried to plug it into the network plug of your PC or laptop? May sound foolish but it fits quite well, offering to a non-experienced user the feeling that it has inserted in the right port (As a user, I was wondering whether this possibility existed until I managed to witness this scenario with my eyes).
Well, nothing happen, luckily, but the user may wonder why his USB mouse is not working anymore, struggling in finding the solution.

Why the standard dimension has been invented so similar to an existing connector? A better Poka-Yoke approach may have avoided this?

Ok, I can imagine what you are thinking, but stay away from giving the fault to the user side. This approach is not fixing any issue, as looking for the guilty it is not a solution.

Example #7: Pedestrian Crossings

In some England cities I have noticed that the crossroads are built so the people are forced towards a path which comes face to face with the oncoming traffic, so that each pedestrian is aware from which angle the vehicle traffic is coming. This protects people who are used to walking in countries where traffic keeps to the right side of the road, avoiding situations in which their instincts are to check the opposite direction for the arrival of vehicles which may lead to a serious risk of an accident.

In the cases I've seen, at the center of the road pedestrians who are crossing are forced to walk a few meters heading left by the dedicated path. This is sufficient to stimulate the attention of the crossing crowd and in many cases avoids the danger of distraction.

A less effective countermeasure and therefore not a Poka-Yoke example is also represented by the writings on the curb indicating to the people which is the direction the vehicles will approach from.

This is not very effective as writing something is definitely not an adequate resolution, as we have already seen in the countermeasures chapter.

Requirement: to cross the street safely also for pedestrians from countries where cars travel on the different side of the road.
Potential error: driven by habits, pedestrians may check for oncoming vehicles on the opposite side to where vehicles arrive from.
Solution: forcing pedestrians to walk into a short section of a crossing facing traffic path, forcing people to realise the traffic direction.

Example #8: Public Baths

To prevent people from forgetting their jackets or vests in public bathrooms, some airports have installed hangers directly above the handle to open the door.

In this way, when the user wants to exit the bathroom, they reach towards the door handle and are forced to move the jacket or coat, avoiding the possibility of leaving the garment behind in the bathroom.

This principle is similar to that of the cash point machines, we can force the user to acknowledge the situation before we allow him to do the activity he has in mind at that particular time.

Requirement: use the bathrooms in public places without forgetting your jacket or coat.
Potential error: forget your coat or raincoat hanging in the bathroom.
Solution: Prevent the handle to exit the bathroom from being reached without removing the coat or raincoat from the hanger.

Example #9: Cruise Ship Bathrooms

On certain cruise ships, passengers complained about the bad smell of bathrooms in their cabins. The analysis of the problem led the ferry company to locate the habit of not lowering the water closet cover to prevent odors.

However it is not possible to prevent all users from learning at their own expenses that this activity is required, taking into account the temporary stay (the cruise lasts a few days) on board ships.

The solution to educate everyone on their arrival to the cabin is expensive as well as less desirable because of the topic, and therefore has developed a Poka-Yoke system to fix the issue: The button to drain the water has been placed on the back wall to the toilet, in a position so low that is not reachable without closing the cover in the horizontal position first.

In this way claims of odors were eliminated. Whoever does not close the toilet seat will not flush away the water so he cannot complain of odors caused by a bathroom left dirty by himself.

Requirement: enjoy the convenience of having a bathroom in the cabin for the gentlemen guests on a cruise ship
Potential error: forgetting to close the toilet seat and cover and consequently experiencing bad odors
Solution: being able to drain the water away only by forcing the user to lower the toilet seat cover.

Example #10: Pay by Card

In all well-made payment systems the payment card must be removed before you can proceed (on the highway, at the gas station, at the ATM, etc.).

Why this does not happen in stores? When you pay with your card on terminals in shops or restaurants, it is the duty of the customer and operator to remember to give back the payment card to the owner at the end of the transaction. Why has this system not been improved?

I personally keep the wallet in my hand until the card is returned to me, in order to have my own personal signal that something is not as expected if it should happen that I walk away with the wallet still in my hand, which among other things prevents me from collecting the shopping-bags of the stuff I have bought.

I also found out that someone has invented a buzzer that sounds until the card is not returned in the wallet. Error proof!

Requirement: using the payment system via magnetic card devices.
Potential error: to leave behind the payment card inside the shop or in the automatic payment machine.
Solution: prevent completion of the transaction until the user has withdrawn their card from the ATM.

Example #11: Hospital Injectable Supplies

In all hospitals the physiological liquids to be injected into the circulatory system of the patient comes already properly diluted to avoid problems related to bad dosages or dilutions.

Similarly, the gases that are delivered bedside the bed of the patient have specific plugs so there can be no mistake in attaching the correct gas, which may also impact safety of the patient.

In this case also the standard color system helps the staff not to waste time in attempts to proceed expeditiously when the need to supply the correct gas.

In some diseases the early intervention is critical to the patient's life.

Requirement: supplying injectable liquids to provide treatments or nutrients to patients in hospitals.
Potential error: wrong dosage can create problems for the patient's health or, at worst, kill them.
Solution: to provide hospital liquids already diluted and gases with specific dilution and connections so that no one can make incorrect dosages.

Example #12: American School Buses

There are school buses in the United States equipped with a special system mounted on the front bumper. During the loading and unloading of children a bar extends hindering the passage of the children in the near proximity of the front part of the vehicle.

These buses have a protruding hood that prevents the driver from seeing what's happening in the immediate vicinity of the front bumper.

Thanks to this mechanism, the children are forced to cross the road by moving away from the front edge of the vehicle, away enough so the driver can see them and wait for their transit before leaving.

Requirement: letting the students leave the bus safely.
Potential error: the driver may not notice that students are placed in front of the vehicle and could move the bus on when students have not yet cleared out of the space in front of the bus.
Solution: to not allow anybody to stay in the immediate proximity of the front of the bus, allowing the driver to see if they are crossing the street in front of the bus, before moving on with the vehicle.

Example #13: Barriers Outside Schools

On the sidewalks in front of certain schools there are barriers installed to prevent children from directly walking into the road when they exit from the school.

As we all may remember, the sound of the bell at the end of the school day corresponds to a time of celebration, which for many means running enthusiastically out of school, to play and have fun with happy activities.

Knowing that Poka-Yoke is effective in all cases in which the carelessness of the person cannot allow them to handle all possible errors, it is important to block every easy access to the road directly in front of the exit of the school, forcing the children to run out in a certain part in their vehemence before ending up under the wheels of some cars.

Requirement: to make sure that the arrival and the exit from the schools are moments in which children can move safely.
Potential error: not being able to predict the movements of all children in front of the school gates, with the danger that some may enter the road while vehicles are passing and may collide with them.
Solution: limit and prevent the possibility that, in the proximity to entrances of the schools, the kids may have free and direct access to the area of the road dedicated to vehicular traffic.

Example #14: Computer Messages

Computerised systems are often rich Poka-Yoke solutions.
For example there are plenty of messages like "are you sure you really want to do this activity?" This question happens in case of action that could result in loss of data, while other messages may force the user through a sequence of steps that must be followed in order to continue, like accepting the license agreements, or entering the required data before allowing the users to proceed.

In these messages computers are far more effective than the check lists, as they prevent totally the user from continuing with the activities in the absence of mandatory and/or proper handling of the data.

Moreover, some controls allow you to avoid typos, like asking for entering two times a certain value. In these cases, only the copy and paste of the value entered as first would stumble into the problem; anyway, if we realise the utility of these systems, we should always re-enter the field and not use copy and paste feature. As the system is there to help us, we should not evade it voluntarily.

Requirement: let the user autonomously make proper use of the systems offered by modern IT technologies.
Potential error: allow the users to fall into certain types of errors that are dangerous for the system itself or for the data.
Solution: before allowing a potentially dangerous action, warn the user with intrusive messages. Moreover, lock some possibilities for non-expert users and for non-system administrators.

Example #15: The Shoe Method

Also in the daily personal activities we can behave to avoid distraction errors.

If we want not to forget a certain object at home or at the office, when it's time for us to go, we should identify what we absolutely cannot forget (like car keys, mobile phone, jacket, etc..) and then physically couple the objects we might forget with those unforgettable ones (like putting your car keys in the envelope with the document that you absolutely need to have with you).

In this way you will not be able to get away if you do not bring with you the things you could eventually forget to take.

If the object cannot be physically coupled to the car keys or jacket, you can always make a note on the car keys in order to remind you when it is time to use them, at the latest.

This is also known as the "shoe method" to remember that if you put an object you cannot forget into your shoes, you will definitely remember it at the time you put on your shoes before heading out. It works unless you decide to go out with another pair of shoes.

Requirement: leaving without the items that we have to carry with us.
Potential error: forgetting a few items before leaving the place where we are.
Solution: to create a physical link between objects that you definitely need to take and those you may forget to take.

Example #16: The Fly

Perhaps it is not a Poka-Yoke solution, but it shows how you can use the taste of a challenge to drive some human behaviour.

There are airports in which toilets address the fact that the urinals gets dirty very quickly.

They draw fake black flies on the white ceramic surface, so that the fake bug proves very visible, mostly positioned at the point where it is useful to direct the urine to not make everything dirty.

This simple trick, leveraging the widespread urge to get into challenges by the male gender, has allowed to significantly reduce the cases in which users were hitting the wrong "target", contributing to the overall cleanliness of the bathrooms.

Requirement: allowing many people to use clean and decent public toilets.
Potential error: to allow people to dirty the bathrooms due to little attention or little respect for those who come after.
Solution: encourage people to behave properly by challenging them through a game of skills

Example #17: Cold Labels

Maybe it has not spread to bad faith or perhaps it's because of the reliability of the warning, but you should know that already in the decade of the 1990's, labels were invented for the frozen foods boxes to ensure the maintenance of the cold chain?

These foods, which should reach the store shelf without ever getting close to the ice fusion temperature, if labeled with this label they would have signaled to the consumer in an unequivocal way that the goods have not followed the cold chain process in their distribution chain from the manufacturer to the shelves of the store.

Requirement: to ensure that the consumer frozen foods have been properly processed and distributed through the entire supply chain in accordance with the minimum storage temperature.
Potential error: to pick up from the refrigerator at the store packages that can be harmful to our health, as they have not followed the cold chain process during distribution.
Solution: give the buyer the opportunity to check whether the packages were stored properly until the time of their purchase.

Example #18: The Orange Network Cable

In a meeting room of a company, a network cable coloured in orange is installed to power and connects the teleconference hands-free phone. Other networking cables in light gray were available for connecting laptops users to the LAN.
On a day in which the connection to the LAN did not seem to be working, the orange wire was tested by plugging it into a laptop (successfully, as it had the same plug network connector) with the result of irreparable electrocute from the network card of the computer, which then has to be replaced.

Following the intervention of the IT department to replace the burned out network card, it was explained that the orange cable is a power cable as well (as requested by the conference hands free phone) while the gray cables are not powered as the computer has other power supplies, so they do not burn the network card of the laptop.
As a solution an e-mail has been sent to attendees of the meeting room to warn them about the problem. Could this have been done better?
Sending an e-mail is not a Poka-Yoke solution and is communication only. New recruits, for example, will not receive any notice and will not be aware of this problem. It is best to fix a notice on the cable at the point where any mistake could happen in the future? Or change the type and shape of the plugs (if this could be done)?

Requirement: use safely the cables available in the meeting room for all operations dedicated to the connectivity of computers and phones.
Potential error: to use the powered network cable in a device that would not support the electrical shock, damaging it, as in the case of the network card in your computer.
Solution: prevent the same cable from being used , identify the dangerous cable not only by color, but also with messages and symbols that clearly demonstrate the use to which it is intended.

Example #19: The Automatic Transmission

The gearshift lever of those cars equipped with automatic transmission cannot be put in the Drive position if you do not press the brake pedal before the operation. The same happens to the modern car that have electric stationary brakes operated by a button.

This ensures that, at the moment in which the car will no longer be "braked" by the Parking position or the stationary brake, it cannot move on a slope of the road inadvertently or because the driver suddenly presses the accelerator pedal.

If you think about it, this action also forces the driver to align properly with the pedals before starting a potentially dangerous operation such as the drive of a vehicle.

Requirement: safely operating the gear selector of automatic cars.
Potential error: operating the lever without paying attention and being surprised by the sudden moving of the car.
Solution: forcing the user to press the brake pedal before allowing him to select a gear starting from the Parking braked position.

Example #20: Brake to Start

Motorised scooters, as well as automobiles, contain many proof distraction expedients, as these vehicles are even more dangerous.

Upon ignition of the bike, if you do not pull the brake levers the scooter does not supply power to the ignition system.

In this way you cannot start the bike without ensuring the bike is braked in an attempt to start the engine.

Requirement: To switch on the motor scooter in a safe way.
Potential error: to accelerate during the operation, triggering the transmission to the rear wheel and having the scooter moving inadvertently.
Solution: forcing the user to apply the brake during the ignition phase.

Example #21: The Bike Side Stand

Another device that is installed on motorcycles is the sensor to monitor the opening of the side stand. If the driver attempt to move with the side stand open, it would be a matter of moments before he would be thrown from the motorcycle by the side stand which hits the ground when the vehicle begins to lean to that side, at the first corner.

A simple switch that detects the opening of the stand is responsible for turning off the engine when the driver tries to engage a gear other than Neutral, thus avoiding a potential injury.

Requirement: safe driving of the motorcycle.
Potential error: moving on leaving the side stand of the bike open with the danger of falling off.
Solution: to automatically turn the engine off if it detects an attempt to insert the gear but the side stand has not closed yet.

Example #22: Industrial Presses

The industrial presses are often operated manually by the operators, or are automated but there is the need for the operator to work with their hands in close proximity to areas in motion.

Unfortunately these machines are very dangerous, so the risk of crushing and amputation is very high.

For this reason, the manually operated presses may only be activated by pushing two buttons at the same time, one in each hand; quite far from each other so that you cannot press both with one arm and with the use of other tricks to keep one hand free at the risk of being amputated.

Requirement: operate safely manual presses.
Potential error: getting too close with a part of the body to the area where the mechanical parts of the press move.
Solution: equip the presses with two buttons to operate, far enough from each other in order to protect both hands and avoid the press from being operated without keeping the hands of the operator in a safe zone.

Example #23: Laser Barriers

In the machine workshops it is not so uncommon to safely protect the operators with infrared barriers; these invisible barriers block the movement of the machine when the barrier is crossed by a body or an object.

This approach can prevent hazardous movements of people who might be injured by coming into contact with moving parts, as well as physical protection, keeping them free.

In other cases it is possible to install a carpet capable of detecting the presence of the operator, ensuring that the machine will not start if the operator or operators are not in a safe place, interrupting the operation by anybody moving away from the safe zone.

Requirement: allow operators to work in the proximity of dangerous machinery without the risk of being injured.
Potential error: allowing the operator to perform unsafe interactions with the machinery.
Solution: turn off the machine automatically in situations where the operator is not safe.

Example #23: The Parking Maneuver

Cars and vehicle in general are always a good source of applied solutions.

Let's think about the parking sensors, or the rear view cameras, or the rods mounted on the bumper or the side mirrors that automatically dim and shows the image of the wheel when the car switches into reverse; all these systems allow you to perceive accurately the dimensions of the vehicle you're driving.

In the parking maneuver, especially when done in confined spaces, all these measures are useful to avoid damages to the vehicle.

Requirement: to allow the maneuvers of vehicles in tight spaces without damaging things or people.
Potential error: leaving uniquely to the driver the task of perceiving the overall dimensions of the vehicle, even in areas where the shape of the vehicle cannot be fully perceived from the driver's point of view.
Solution: to amplify the perception of the surrounding space to the driver, facilitating him to maneuver without bumping into obstacles.

Example #24: Seatbelts

The combination between cars and safety has made a lot of progresses in the Poka-Yoke direction. Systems, lights or sounds to warn passengers of a vehicle that their seat belt is not correctly fastened are now common on all cars.

The effectiveness of these solutions lies primarily in the annoying loudness and tone they create so the passenger is incentivised to wear seat belts properly.

In this, as in other cases, sharing the pain motivates people to change their attitude.

Requirements: to have the occupants of vehicles properly wearing the seatbelts.
Potential error: forgetting or voluntarily not wearing the seatbelt.
Solution: warn the occupants of the vehicle by means of sound systems that, in addition to being easily audible, may contribute to worsening the comfort of the journey, so as to encourage travelers to choose the less annoying compromise, which is to wear the seat belt.

Open Question: could it be a more effective signal which is visible from outside the vehicle when the occupants are not wearing the belt?
This would be effective on people who try to be clever just because they are not seen and would help the police to identify those who do not respect the rules of the road. Alternatively, this could be effective to make sure that the vehicle does not ignite or just moves with a limitation of performance when the occupants are wearing seat belts properly?

Obviously, exceptions should be managed for specific categories that may have special permissions to travel without wearing the seatbelt.

Example #25: An Additional Eye

In the automotive field, not only can parking maneuver harm people and objects, but also during the movements while driving.

Here as well, thanks to statistics on the most common errors, some solutions have been applied to help the driver.

Certain cars are equipped with devices to detect the presence of obstacles that could interfere with the operations that are being made, such as systems that signal the presence of a vehicle to the left of your car, in the so-called "dead zone" of the side mirror, lighting a LED or transmitting a vibration to the steering wheel of drivers who show the intention to change lane by using the indicator.

Other systems help to maintain the same lane thanks to cameras which monitor the lines on the ground that mark the lanes; these systems transmit sound or vibration feedbacks to the steering wheel for those who are driving should they tend to drive outside of the lane.

Other examples are radar monitoring systems of the distance kept from the preceding vehicle, which are programmed to operate the brakes if they deem a possible impact, in order to limit as much as possible the consequences of the collision.

These systems are not very welcome by the drivers as such mechanisms tend to apply the brakes even in undesired circumstances. There are situations in which the drivers are willing to approach the car they are following, to gain the extra speed required to rapidly overtake it; in such cases the system may create additional danger as applies the brakes in the same moment in which the drivers are changing lane to overtake the other car, and this unexpected behaviour in such moment is something undesirable.
Studying the consequences of the countermeasures may become

a good approach to avoid additional issues may derive from the countermeasure itself.

Requirement: allow the driver to operate the vehicle in traffic in conditions with a high degree of safety.
Potential error: as a result of distraction or poor visibility, to maneuver in such a way that may lead to collisions with other vehicles.
Solution: add dynamic monitoring systems which pick up the position of the vehicle relative to other vehicles and to the conformation of the road, so as to increase the perception of the driver up to activating the braking system to reduce the consequences of imminent impacts.

Example #26: Release the Brake!

In modern cars, thanks to the invention of electronics, it has been possible to easily implement a mechanism for interrupting the engine power in some cases where this is not appropriate or dangerous.

We start from the case in which the driver presses the accelerator and brake at the same time (the power is cut and the result is a readily understandable error by the driver, and it works as well as an interruption of the process that can damage the vehicle or cause it to wear early).

Also the traction and/or stability control makes use of the same approach to cut power. In normal use the system monitors the rotation of the wheels for abnormal situations and intervenes by cutting power to the motor if it the wheel rotation is abnormal and may cause a loss of grip with the ground.

Requirement: to allow the driver to exploit the full power of the engine without incurring inappropriate behaviour that could damage the vehicle or make him lose the control.
Potential error: accidentally pressing the brake pedal together with the accelerator, or providing excessive power in relation to the grip of the road surface.
Solution: add to the engine software system the program to reduce the available power in abnormal situations.

Example #27: Drink or Drive

A French law introduced a mandatory device for all the buses and coaches so that the engine can be switched on only by having the driver blowing into a Breathalyzer (a device that detects the alcohol content of the human blood).

In this way they help fight against who is driving while drunk, if the alcohol content is above the legal limit, the device prevents the engine from being switched on.

However, these systems are easily by-passed in cases, for example, in which who starts the engine of the bus may be a different person from the one who is then sat behind the steering wheel.

Similar countermeasures are by-passable by the users; therefore require subsequent effort in monitoring the situations to catch up with whoever is not respecting the law, applying even higher fines because it is no more a matter of distraction.

Requirement: increase safety of road users who rely on professional transportation to a higher degree by intercepting and blocking the ability to drive buses by drunk drivers as per law's limits.
Potential error: traveling on a bus driven by a person who may have exceeded the alcohol limit.
Solution: avoid starting the engine of the bus if the person who attempts to drive does not prove to have a blood-alcohol rate below the maximum allowed limit.

Example #28: Cooking without Explosions

Many home kitchens are equipped with a system, mandatory in many countries, which interrupts the flow of gas to the stove if the flame does not stay lit. In this system, a temperature sensor (thermocouple) when is lapped by the lit flame, maintains the flow of gas.

If the flame is extinguished, the sensor would detect this within a short time because the temperature is too low, stopping the flow of gas before it saturates into the environment and results in a risk of asphyxiation or explosion.

Requirement: to allow cooking and food preparation in safe conditions.
Potential error: creating a risk of asphyxiation or explosion consequently to an extinguished flame (with continuous leakage of gas) as a result of air movement or leakage of liquids from the pots.
Solution: add a temperature sensor to the gas supply system so that the gas is automatically stopped in cases where the flame does not touch the sensor anymore.

12. CONCLUSIONS

Goal	Share with the reader some conclusions on the method APS
Content  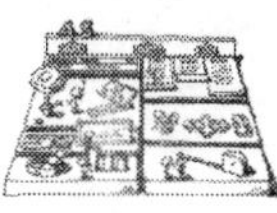	• Final Considerations

Final Considerations

We have said this in the opening, now let's repeat it in the closing: to own a problem solving method has an enormous potential and can contribute in giving us an edge in the early stages of analysis, to understand what is happening.
Even more important, however, is the care of the execution side of the solutions, which usually makes the difference between those who just speak and those who make the problem disappearing.

If we think of how many people speak and continue just to talk about solutions, we do agree that it is probably better to use the skills that we have improved to do something different, is more valuable. Should we talk less and not complain about the past, then we can think about what can be done today to avoid the problem tomorrow.
Finally, once solutions are identified, we have to do everything to ensure their effectiveness, proving to others that we have the rare gift of "making things happen".

Our leadership will emerge much stronger, the people we deal with will begin to recognise some effectiveness in doing the right things at the right time, with personal satisfaction; we will be taken as an example and when we talk we'll have our own audience and chance to influence positively their behaviour.

In job interviews, regardless of the side of the table where we sit, we will have a very clear idea about the skills of the professional profiles. We can ascertain the level of the candidates very easily if we act as interviewers, it will be very easy to prove our skills if we got interviewed as candidates. On all other occasions, including less formal situations, we will have something extra to contribute towards the success of our working group, as well as our personal success.

In the next pages you will find some simple references to the

APS method, the complete APS Doughnut, APS and the graphical representation of the A3 as well as a simple checklist to help yourself in verifying the completeness of each APS step before proceeding with the next step.
Simple but effective guidelines that you may photocopy or just have as picture on your smartphone, and bring with you to use as a reference in your future problem-solving activities.

Have a good Problem Solving!

Ivan

Page intentionally left blank

The APS Methodology

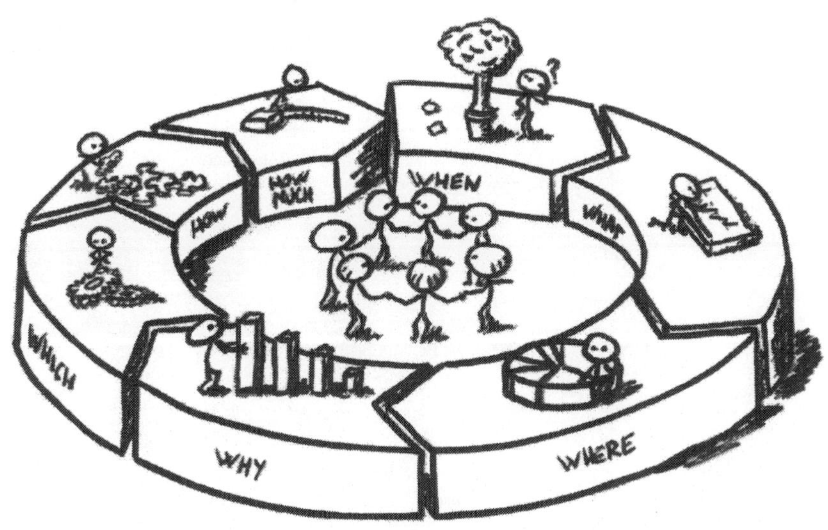

The A3 Form, a Problem Solving Canvas

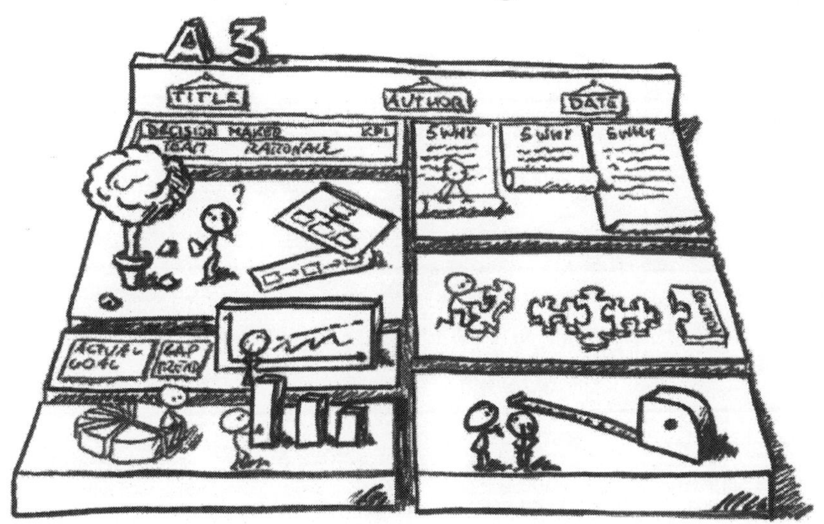

Checklist

WHEN:	✓ **THE ARROW OF TIME:** reorganise the evidence based on the moment in time in which they occurred ✓ **THE PROBLEM TREE:** understand the complexity of the scenario and identify how to measure the problem
WHAT: RUN CHART	✓ **STATEMENT:** Clearly define the statement of the problem (2 lines, quantitative evaluations) ✓ **TEAM:** Identify the team, the team leader and who to involve ✓ **OWNER:** Identify the accountable owner for the Problem Solving ✓ **RATIONALE:** Explain the Rationale ✓ **METRICS:** Identify the Actual, Goal, Gap and Trend ✓ **RUN CHART:** Plot the metrics in a chart
WHERE: GEMBA	✓ **PIE:** identify the most significant Gemba where to conduct the investigations (places, times, types, families, etc.). ✓ **GO TO GEMBA:** physically go to Gemba to use the senses
WHY:	✓ **PARETO:** represent the most important causes ✓ **KEEP IT SIMPLE:** work only on the vital few main causes ✓ **5 WHY:** one 5why analysis for each bar of the Pareto histogram ✓ **UOM:** stick to the rule on units of measure ✓ **$:** jumping to money resolution is forbidden
WHICH: M.I.N.	✓ **MIN:** investigate and identify the process which is Missing, Incomplete or not followed ✓ **ROOT CAUSE:** is one of the processes responsible for the Gap
HOW: PLAN DO! FORGET EVALUATE	✓ **BRAINSTORM:** leverage and exploit the ideas of everybody ✓ **OPPORTUNITY MATRIX:** select the most effective solutions ✓ **POKA-YOKE:** develop ideas into Poka-Yoke solutions
HOW MUCH:	✓ **HOW MUCH:** Identify how to measure the applied solutions
SUSTAIN:	✓ **30-60-90:** monitor at regular intervals the sustainability and effectiveness of the solutions

13. BIOGRAPHY

Goal	Share with the reader the author's biographical traits
Content	• Biographical Notes

Biographical Notes

Ivan Fantin was born in Milan in 1973, where he lives and works, returning from different and interesting experiences in Europe and America.

He is happily married and has two beautiful daughters.

In his childhood falls in love with sports, starting with 5 years of Judo and continuing with over 20 years of Ice and In-Line Hockey championships. In recent years, the love for running appeared so he decide to train constantly to stay healthy and to measure and improve himself on the marathon distance.

In the period between twenty and thirty years he has coached different Ice Hockey teams, from junior to senior categories, male and female groups, competing in Italian and Swiss leagues, accumulating significant experience in managing groups and working to targets.

Having the Master's degree conquered with a full score in science subjects in the academic year 1999 at the State University of Milan, he began his professional career as a consultant for corporate quality systems and ISO 9000 certifications.

After about a year and a half he choose to deepen and broaden the analysis and reviews of the business flows moving into the Operations and IT fields, collecting six years of international experience in the manufacturing, banking, telecommunication, food and pharmaceutical industries, with the role of Project Manager, Account Manager and finally Program Manager.

In the early stages of the next phase of his career, more than six years of employment within the Medical Devices Group of Danaher Corporation (NYSE: DHR), he devotes himself to the study and the application of lean manufacturing and continuous improvement of business processes. It is in this long evolution towards the challenge of a deeper and deeper reviews of business processes he consolidates the knowledge about the techniques for managing the changes in typical corporate cultures.

In this phase, with an increasing interest in managing the consensus around the organisational changes, he develops his own approach in conducting problem solving coaching sessions and, in general, problem solving applied skills, one of the pillars of successful managers.

Ivan is an MBB, CPIM and PMP certified professional; he currently works to continuously improve business processes within the CIRCOR Group (NYSE: CIR), regularly delivers public speeches, writes articles, performs problem solving training and coaching sessions, as well as problem solving workshops, both within the group and in collaboration with external organisations.

Page intentionally left blank

14. BIBLIOGRAPHY

Goal	Provide references to key texts that influenced the writing of this book.

- AAVV, *Business Model Generation: a handbook for visionaries, game changers and challengers,* Wiley and Sons, 2010
- AAVV, *Strategic Management of Resources. Participant Workbook v2.3.* APICS The Association for Operations Management, 2013
- Alberto Galgano, *TOYOTA. Perché l'industria italiana non progredisce,* Guerini e Associati, 2005
- C.M. Cipolla, *Allegro ma non troppo,* Ed. Il Mulino, 1988
- Dan Roam, *The Back of the Napkin,* Penguin Books, 2009
- David Sibbet, *Visual Meetings: How Graphics, Sticky Notes and Idea Mapping can transform group productivity,* Wiley and Sons, 2010
- Ethan Rasiel, Paul Friga, *The McKinsey Mind: Understanding and Implementing the Problem-Solving Tools and Management Techniques of the World's Top Strategic Consulting Firm*, McGraw-Hill, 2001.
- James P. Womack, Daniel T. Jones, *Lean thinking. Banish Waste and Create Wealth in Your Corporation,* Free Press, 2003
- Jeffrey K. Liker, *The Toyota Way. 14 Management Principles from the World's Greatest Manufacturer,* Mcgraw - Hill, 2003
- Jeffrey K. Liker, David Meier, *The Toyota Way Fieldbook: A Practical Guide For Implementing Toyota's 4Ps*, Mcgraw - Hill, 2005
- Jeffrey K. Liker, Gary L. Convis, *The Toyota Way to Lean Leadership: Achieving and Sustaining Excellence Through Leadership Development,* McGraw-Hill, 2011
- John A. Paulos, *Innumeracy: Mathematical illiteracy and its consequences,* Hill & Wang Pub. 2001
- John Shook, *A3 Managing to Learn: Using the A3 Management Process,* Lean Enterprise Institute, 2008
- Leandro Herrero, *Homo Imitans. The art of social infection: viral change in action,* Meeting Minds Publishing, 2011
- Mike Rother, *Toyota Kata: Managing People for*

Improvement, Adaptiveness, and Superior Results, McGraw-Hill, 2009

- Nassim N. Taleb, *The Black Swan. The Impact of the Highly Improbable,* Random House Inc., 2010
- Shigeo Shingo, *Non-Stock Production,* Productivity Press, 1988
- Slack et al., *Operations and Process Management,* Pearson Education, 2009
- Taiichi Ohno, *Toyota Production System. Beyond Large-Scale Production*, Productivity Press, 1988
- The Productivity Press Development Team, *Mistake-Proofing for Operators: The ZQC System,* CRC Press, 1997
- Thompson et al., *Crafting & Executing Strategy,* McGraw-Hill, 15th edition
- Tiziano Villa, *Management By Project,* Ipsoa, 2008
- Wason P.C., *On the failure to eliminate hypotheses in a conceptual task.* Quarterly Journal of Experimental Psychology, 12, 1960
- Willy Apply, *I dodici sensi,* Associazione Amici della Scuola Steineriana, Scuola Rudolf Steiner di Milano, 1990

Made in the USA
Lexington, KY
20 May 2015